CONFIDENT COMMUNICATION

CONFIDENT COMMUNICATION

THE ESSENTIAL SKILLS AND HABITS OF INFLUENTIAL COMMUNICATORS

Published 2025 by Gildan Media LLC
aka G&D Media
www.GandDmedia.com

CONFIDENT COMMUNICATION. Copyright © 2025 by Pryor Learning, LLC. All rights reserved.

No part of this book may be used, reproduced or transmitted in any manner whatsoever, by any means (electronic, photocopying, recording, or otherwise), without the prior written permission of the author, except in the case of brief quotations embodied in critical articles and reviews. No liability is assumed with respect to the use of the information contained within. Although every precaution has been taken, the author and publisher assume no liability for errors or omissions. Neither is any liability assumed for damages resulting from the use of the information contained herein.

Front cover design by David Rheinhardt of Pyrographx

Interior design by Meghan Day Healey of Story Horse, LLC

Library of Congress Cataloging-in-Publication Data is available upon request

ISBN: 978-1-7225-0731-2

10 9 8 7 6 5 4 3 2 1

CONTENTS

FOREWORD 7

ONE
Mastering Communication Skills
— 9 —

TWO
Enhancing Emotional Intelligence
— 35 —

THREE
Active Listening Skills
— 67 —

FOUR
Managing Emotions in the Workplace
— 95 —

FIVE
Confronting Workplace Conflict
— 129 —

SIX
Great Grammar and Painless Proofreading
— 161 —

SEVEN
Bad Email Habits
— 187 —

EIGHT
Business Writing and Editing
— 217 —

CONCLUSION 241

FOREWORD

Pryor Learning has been at the forefront of corporate training, shaping the skills and careers of millions. Founded more than fifty years ago, when Fred Pryor pioneered the "one-day seminar," Pryor Learning has become one of the nation's leading training providers, offering efficient, affordable, and accessible career education for business professionals. Our diverse offerings cater to a wide array of individuals and organizations alike, from small and mid-sized businesses to governments, nonprofits, and Fortune 500 companies.

Offering thousands of in-person seminars annually, Pryor Learning is synonymous with practical, hands-on training that delivers results. As the workforce continues to evolve, so do we—embracing new technologies and expanding our reach. Today we offer a vast array of training options including in-person, live virtual, and on-demand formats, all designed to meet the diverse needs of a constantly changing workplace.

This book, and the series it belongs to, represents the next step in our mission to empower professionals with the essential skills they need to excel. In response to the growing popularity of e-books and audiobooks, we aim to reach a new generation of learners, equipping them with the tools and knowledge to thrive in their careers. Our goal remains simple: to uphold Fred Pryor's legacy by making high-quality business training accessible to all, regardless of where they are in their career journey.

Join us in a tradition of learning that spans more than fifty years—a tradition that has empowered millions to achieve their professional goals. We invite you to explore the wealth of knowledge contained within these pages, knowing that you are part of something greater—a community dedicated to continuous growth and improvement.

This volume of the series, *Confident Communication*, will explore effective communication. Its importance cannot be understated. Verbal and nonverbal communication are critical skills in every successful workplace—at the team and employee level—as well as in your personal relationships.

Learning how to communicate clearly and professionally is key to organizational growth, longevity, and productivity. It is essential for deescalating tense situations, dealing with difficult employees, enhancing emotional intelligence, and listening effectively to your significant other. This compelling, idea-packed book will help you will learn how to communicate with others in an assertive yet nonthreatening and sensitive way.

One important point to note at the outset: nothing in this book should be construed as legal advice. If you have a specific question of a legal nature, please consult your attorney.

ONE

Mastering Communication Skills

In your business career, you will have any number of opportunities to meet people and make new contacts. It's wise to make as much of those opportunities as you possibly can, but you've got only one chance to make a great first impression. In this chapter, we're going to talk about how to make great first impressions and add credibility when you're talking to your boss, colleagues, and customers.

This chapter will begin by discussing how to craft a clear verbal message. It will go on to recovering from faux pas, the unspoken rules of business etiquette, the basic skills of networking, and giving productive criticism and feedback. You will also learn to read faces and look at subtle clues to what someone is really saying as well as how to remember names at initial meetings. Finally, we'll address some of the dos and don'ts of your workspace.

The SEER Method

At some point in your career (if you haven't already), you're going to be in a meeting with your boss or upper-level management. Or maybe you'll be on a job interview and somebody asks you, "What do you think? What are your thoughts?" You'll need to make your point clearly and concisely without getting wordy; otherwise your hearers will lose track and you'll lose your credibility.

One way of making a point effectively is the *SEER method*. It's a very simple template. It stands for *summary, expand, example,* and *restate*.

Summary   **E**xpand   **E**xample   **R**estate

1. **Summary.** Share your opinion in one sentence.
2. **Expand.** Say why you feel this way.
3. **Example.** This is where you add credibility to your point.
4. **Restate.** Repeat the message delivered in your summary.

With a summary, you state your opinion in one sentence at the outset and restate it at the end. With the expansion, you explain why you feel this way, and the example adds credibility.

Let's look at three different types of example: (1) a very simple everyday conversation; (2) a more controversial situation; and (3) communicating with your boss.

Let's start with something very simple. Let's say your spouse asks you where you think you should vacation next fall. Your answer is, "I think we should vacation in the Smoky

Mountains. I love it up there." Is that your opinion? Sure. Does it have a lot of credibility? No.

What if you use the SEER method? Summary: "I think we should vacation in the Smoky Mountains." Now expand: why do you think this way? "It's a great time of year to visit up there, especially in the fall. For example, the average temperature is 50 degrees and there's some snow up in the mountains. That's one reason I think we should go to the Smokies."

In real time, it would sound something like this: "I think we should go to the Smoky Mountains next fall. It's a great time of year to visit. For example, the average temperature is fifty degrees, and there's some snow up in the mountains. That's one reason I love the Smokies in the fall."

Which example adds more credibility? The first one—"I just like the Smokies"—or the second one? Most people would agree that the second one is far more credible.

Now let's talk about something a little bit more controversial. Maybe something like politics or mask mandates, something that people feel very strongly about. Now let's say that you have a neighbor named Richard, and you ask him, "Who are you going to vote for as mayor of Pensacola this year?"

Richard says, "I'm going to vote for Mrs. Smith. I just like her. She's great." Is that Richard's opinion? Sure it is. Does it have a lot of credibility to it? Not really. What if Richard had used the SEER method? "I'm going to vote for Mrs. Smith for mayor of Pensacola." Expand, showing why: "I especially like her stance on the environment." Or "I especially like her position on bringing high-paying jobs to our area." Example: "She has a plan to be 25 percent green in her first two years of office." Or "She has a plan to bring 300 new jobs to Pensacola in the next two years." Restate: "That's why I'm going to vote for Mrs. Smith for mayor of Pensacola."

Again, which approach sounds more credible? Saying you're voting for Mrs. Smith because you just like her or using the SEER method? The second is much more credible, because you're saying why you feel this way and are giving an example to back it up.

Now let's consider an example that you could use in a business situation. Let's say you are in a meeting with your boss and another colleague, and the purpose of the meeting is to decide which software your company should buy: software A or software B. The other person says, "I think we should purchase software A because it's cheaper by a thousand bucks." You, however, think you should go with software B.

When you're being persuasive, you need to find out what is important to the person you need to convince. Let's say you work for a call center and your boss is highly motivated by efficiency. She has said that the software has to be easy to use, because you've got some technically challenged employees. Moreover, long-term warranties are really important.

Here is how you make your point. The summary would be, "I think we should purchase software B." Expand by explaining why: "It'll save us time when talking to customers." Give an example to back up your case. For example, "All the information can be seen using one screen. We don't have to toggle back and forth, saving us time." Circle back around with the restate. Another reason is, "It's very easy to use. For example, the manufacturer of software B has a training program where all employees can be up and running within four hours." Then circle back around and expand. "For example, software B comes with a five-year warranty, which covers all defects. The other option only comes with a two-year warranty." Using the SEER method, you state your position, then you explain why, giving examples, and finally you restate your point.

Another example: you're on a job interview and you say, "I think I'm a great candidate for the position." Why? "One reason is that I take the initiative at work." Then you give an example of a situation or situations in the past when you've taken the initiative.

That's the SEER method: state your opinion in one sentence, explain why you feel that way, give an example to prove your point, and then restate it.

Faux Pas

As for recovering from faux pas, when you say something you wish you could take back or you've made a mistake, use simple statements, like:
- "I can't believe I just said that. Please accept my apology."
- "I can't believe I just did that. Please accept my apology."
- "I shouldn't have said that. Please accept my apology."
- "That came out wrong. What I meant to say is this . . ."
- "We all make mistakes, right? Not my best moment."
- If you happen to say or do something to which someone takes offense, you can say, "I didn't mean to offend you. Please accept my apology."

> When you make a faux pas, give a simple apology. Then it's over.

Then it's over. Notice that these statements are not wordy. One or two sentences—that's it.

Instead of apologizing in an email, you might want to consider saying, "Thank you for catching that," or, "I appreciate your bringing this error to my attention." You don't make a big deal out of it. Professionals will say, "Thanks for flagging this for me," and they move on. They don't dwell on the mistakes that they've made. If you're running late for a meeting, instead of saying, "Sorry, I'm late," use positive words: "Thanks for waiting for me."

If someone else makes a mistake, show empathy without overstating. Use simple statements, like, "I can see how that could happen" or, "Mistakes happen, you know." You can also say, "I've made that same mistake myself," or "I'm sure many people have made the same mistake." These statements help the other person bridge from where we are now to where we need to be.

Business Etiquette

Now let's look at some unspoken rules of business etiquette, especially when you're networking, and how to express your identity professionally.

How do you project an impressive image of self-confidence, professionalism, and competency? You get one chance to make a great first impression. How do you fit in with any group of businesspeople, no matter how much or little you have in common?

> ## You get one chance to make a great first impression.

If you are at a networking event, you are there to make business contacts, not to hang out with your friends or coworkers. You already know them. Walk up to somebody you don't know and introduce yourself. That's why they're there; that's why you're there. Just walk up, make eye contact, and keep your shoulders square. Don't turn your body away, because that implies turning away psychologically. Use a firm handshake, not the dead fish. Ask open-ended questions. When you introduce yourself, say your name and where you work. The other person is likely to do the same. Then you can say, "Tell me about that. What do you like about working there?" That's how business conversations get started.

When you are having a conversation, especially in a networking event, be very careful about "autobiographical listening." This happens when the other person is talking about what a tough day they had or how much stress they have at work. When they take a pause, even if they're not done, you jump in and talk about how stressful your day is or how tough you have it at work. Sometimes we do that because we want to relate to what is being said. But the reality is, you just cut that person off.

That is autobiographical listening: when we jump in and interrupt somebody else. If you've ever had that happen to you at a networking event, you know how disrespectful it feels. It's also a lost opportunity.

When you meet a total stranger, ask where they work rather than jumping in and talking about you and about where you work. Ask about their job. Ask what services they use; ask if there are any opportunities there for your own business.

Enter the other person's space and ask open-ended questions. If they talk about what a tough day they're having at work, you can say, "What's stressing you out so much at work? Can you give me some examples?" You're expanding on what they brought up, because it's important to them.

When they're done, you can go ahead and add your own examples of what a tough day you've had or how much stress you're under.

Here are some more tips for networking.

1. **Don't multitask.** This means much more than just putting your cell phone away. It means to be present. When you're conversing with someone, don't think about your boss or work or your long drive home. Be in the conversation.
2. **Don't pontificate.** A conversation is a two-way street. If you don't want to listen to the other person or hear another point of view, write a blog. That way nobody can give you their response. Conversations are back and

forth, listening and using open-ended questions like, "Tell me about that. Can you give me an example?" That opens up dialogue, especially in a business situation.

3. **Go with the flow.** While you're conversing with someone, you need to let ideas come and go. You may hear something that reminds you about a great story that you experienced. You want to jump right in and talk about it, even though it has nothing to do with the conversation. Stay on topic.
4. **If you don't know, say you don't know.** There's nothing wrong with saying, "I don't have that experience," or "I don't know the answer."
5. **Don't equate your experiences with their experiences.** That is definitely a networking no-no. It's a lot like autobiographical listening. If the other person is talking about a serious situation or the stress they have at work, don't jump in and talk about how much you hate your boss. It's not the same. It's never the same. It's about the other person.
6. **Try not to repeat yourself.** Say it once, using the SEER method, and move on.
7. **Stay out of the weeds.** Don't get bogged down with every single detail, because details usually aren't that important. The other person wants to hear about the broad scope of what you're talking about here.
8. **Listen.** We all know about listening skills. Again, avoid autobiographical listening.
9. **Be brief.** Use the SEER method. Make your point; don't talk in circles.

Expressing Your Identity Professionally

It's important to express your identity, but to do it professionally, while projecting an image of self-confidence. You're giving the impression that you are confident, you are professional, and the other person should be talking to you.

Here are some tips.

1. **If you're standing up during a conversation, stand tall; don't slouch.** If you slouch, it looks as if you're sloppy, as if you don't care. Open hands, open arms. Openness means that you're open to the conversation. As for eye contact, you don't have to stare somebody down, but do make eye contact. If that's tough for you, look at the other person's forehead for a couple of seconds and then look down at their chin. Then maybe you'll break away and come back and look at their cheek. This way, it appears that you are making eye contact. You know what it's like to communicate with somebody who's not making eye contact.

2. **Shoulders square towards the other person.** We've already discussed this point.

3. **Just smile.** Have some fun, be pleasant, and smile.

4. **Keep your clothes looking fresh and clean.** There is nothing worse than going to a professional event and seeing somebody who has nice clothes, but they're wrinkled. If you show up with a wrinkled shirt or blouse or pants, it implies that you don't care, and a lot of people will notice that.

5. **Pay attention to your nails.** Manicure them, clip them. Your nails indicate that you're likely to pay attention to details at work. Little things like this make a big difference.

6. **Shoes.** Invest in the best shoes you can possibly afford, not only for comfort, but also because they look professional. You don't want to have a great-looking outfit on with ratty shoes. Keep them polished and scuff-free. If the heels are worn down, get them repaired. Buy cedar shoe trees. They preserve the shape of your shoes, but they also help control odor and actually absorbs moisture. And it is really helpful to keep your shoes polished.

7. **Pay attention to your accessories.** Invest in some useful high-quality accessories. Don't be cheap about this. You don't have to buy a Rolex watch, but carry a decent pen. If you're going to use a briefcase or portfolio, make sure to have a good-looking one, because that speaks volumes about you and your success.

8. **Always carry some business cards as well as a pen.** Especially if you're out networking, you're going to meet somebody you don't know, and they're going to hand you their business card. When the conversation breaks, you can write a couple of notes down on the back of their card: "The person does this at the company," or "Give a follow-up call to this." If you don't have a pen, you're not going to be able to do that. Of course you should give them your business card as well.

9. **Keep a jacket or suit coat—some kind of business attire—handy at all times.** It may be on the back of the chair in your office, or maybe in your car. Protect it with a garment bag. You never know when you'll get a call for a last-minute meeting with a client or customer.

10. **Stay away from clothes that don't look good**: they're too tight, too short, too baggy, too revealing, or they have holes. If you're honestly not sure whether you should wear a particular item or not, don't take the chance, especially in a business situation.

11. **Bring an extra tie, dress shirt, or blouse to a business meeting.** You never know when you're going to spill a little coffee or ketchup on your shirt or tie. Always have a backup.

12. **Use positive expressions.** Instead of saying, "Sorry to interrupt you," use expressions like, "I'd like to add . . ." or "I have an idea," or "I'd like to expand on that." These are much better than "Sorry to interrupt you." Similarly, if you need to make a complaint, rather than saying, "Sorry to complain," you might say, "Thank you for listening." This projects much more of a professional image when you have to bring up a different point of view.

Giving and Receiving Feedback

Now we come to managing anger, conflict, betrayal, toxic personalities, and negativity in a professional work environment.

When you are giving feedback to someone, whether an employee or a coworker, always do so in private, never in public. You never want to embarrass people. If you do, they'll never forget how you made them feel.

> You never want to embarrass people. If you do, they'll never forget how you made them feel.

Furthermore, when you're giving feedback, attack the problem, not the person. You don't say, "You did this." You talk about the issue and the problem and not the person. If you say, "You know, Steve, you are killing this team because you can't hit the deadline," that's personal. Instead, you might say, "When these deadlines are not met, this is how it affects our production schedule." In this case, you're talking about the deadlines. You don't throw in the word "you."

When you're giving feedback, either positive or corrective, be specific; try to use examples. It adds credibility. Also, be timely. Don't wait five months before you give feedback of any kind, because it loses its emphasis.

Finally, focus on the future, not the past. Use the 10/90 rule instead of the 90/10 rule. Many people spend 90 percent of the time talking about the problem—blaming, saying whose fault it is—and only 10 percent of the time talking about solutions. Truly impressive professionals flip the numbers around: they spend 10 percent of the time talking about the problem and 90 percent of the time looking for solutions.

Sometimes you have to get feedback from people, especially somebody who's very angry, and you really don't know how to take it. Don't lose your cool, and stay in control. Suppose your supervisor is stomping towards you, ranting about the month-end figures you gave them yesterday, claiming they're inaccurate and starting to attack you personally. They're saying things like, "Listen, if you don't start shaping up quickly, you might as well look for another job. A two-year-old would spot this mistake you're making." Rather than panicking and saying, "I'll do better, I'll do better," take a breath and ask a question: "I want to correct the problem. What specifically is wrong with my report?" That's it. It may not be the entire report: the boss might just be having a problem with a very small part of it.

Another suggestion: when you are getting feedback, listen before you speak. Seek first to understand and then to be understood. Ask questions; ask for examples. When you don't agree with the feedback, listen for the facts. Ask yourself, is there any possibility that this could be accurate? At least some of it could be accurate. Maybe talk to another person to gain some perspective: "I was told by my boss that I sometimes do this. Have you ever noticed that?" Again, go back to the 10/90 rule: 10 percent focus on the problem, 90 percent on the solution.

When you are dealing with anger, conflict, and toxic personalities in the workplace, you want to always remain professional. You don't want to buy into their emotions and responses.

It's important for you as a business professional to manage the gap between the stimulus and the response. The stimulus is, what happened? Your boss said X; a customer said Y.

How long does it take the limbic system in your brain (which governs your emotions) to come up with a response? Actually, it's less than one second. You're ready to fire off your response immediately. You can recognize this fact if you've ever said anything you wish you could take back.

Instead, when faced with a negative comment or personality, you want to respond rather than reacting, because reaction is driven by emotion. We communicate with our emotions; our responses are driven by rational thought. Here too you want to ask questions: "Give me an example; what do you mean by this?" Then give your response calmly and professionally.

Here is another important point: when there is a problem at work, solve the problem first and deal with the emotions later. Many people are so wrapped up in their emotions and how much it bothers them that they never address the problem. Solve the problem first; deal with the emotions later.

Solve the problem first and deal with the emotions later.

When you are in a professional work environment or just in your life in general, it's wise to put things in perspective. Play the time warp game: When you're getting stressed out or you're under a lot of pressure, ask yourself: one year from now, is this really going to matter? Often people get their emotions wrapped up in issues and problems that are really not going to matter a year from now—or a week from now. Ask yourself: one year from now, is this really going to matter?

When you do have conflict with your boss or a colleague, it is very important to establish common ground. Common ground is what you both agree to; In other words, what do we want the end of this conversation to be? We both want this outcome. How we get there is critically important; in fact, that's usually where the conflict is. We'll say a little more below about the importance of common ground and how to use it.

You may find yourself dealing with people who are very aggressive—confident, loud, overbearing, argumentative, confrontational. Be prepared for these individuals, because you're never going to change them. Speak quietly and firmly. Again, think about common ground. What do you want to accomplish when you communicate with this person? You want to be firm, but try not to get into any confrontation, especially in front of other people.

In arguments, demonstrate that you value their experience and their passion: "Look, I respect the fact that you have a lot of experience in this matter and have a very strong opinion about this." This brings defenses down quite a bit and starts to form common ground.

When you're dealing with an angry person and they're passing blame, use scripts like, "I'm here to find a solution, not to place blame. I'm not going to get into that blame game. Let's fix the problem instead of finding the blame."

Other scripts: Ask, "Would you be open to hearing some more ideas?" or "Can I tell you what I think about this?" or maybe, "Can we synergize on this?" When they agree, that gives you a chance to express your thoughts.

People frequently ask about negative Nelly and negative Ned. There are always going to be people like that in working environments. Never get involved with their negativity. Don't add fuel to the fire by saying, "Yep, yep, yep," because holding people accountable is important. If the negative person is talking about the boss, Mr. Smith, just ask this question: "Have you talked to Mr. Smith about this?" "No." Then your response is right here: "Then I would prefer not to hear about it until you've talked to Mr. Smith." It's not confrontational; you're simply saying, "I don't need to be hearing this. I don't want to hear the gossip about the boss until you've actually addressed it with him or her."

Remembering Names and Faces

Have you ever had this happen to you? You've just met a business contact and you've exchanged names, and then five seconds later you've totally forgotten their name. Another situation: you meet someone for the first time at a business function and you talk for quite a while, but you don't see the person for several months. One day you run into them at some unusual place, like the bank or the grocery store, and they remember your name. They ask questions about your family and your business. You have no idea who they are, even though they look familiar.

Remembering information about people is not about memorization: it's about recall. If you've heard the person's name, it's in your brain. Can you recall it, though, when you need it?

Let's review some quick tips on remembering people's names and other information. Never think or say, "I'm just bad with names." That's a cheap excuse, meaning, "I'm not even going to try to remember the person's name." Instead, use a positive approach: "I'm great with names. I will remember this person's name." When you meet somebody, "I'm going to remember their name." It's amazing how far a positive attitude goes in helping you remember people's names.

> Never think or say, "I'm just bad with names."
> That's a cheap excuse.

Other simple steps: When you meet a business contact for the first time, catch the name first. When you meet someone, get everything else outside your mind for the first five or six seconds, because their name is coming. Don't be thinking about what you're wearing or what you're going to say. Think of catching their name.

If you don't catch their name for whatever reason—maybe you didn't understand it; maybe you just missed it—ask for it again right away. When you introduce yourself to someone; you don't want to miss their name only to have them remember yours, so you're thinking for five minutes, "I hope somebody mentions their name." Don't do it. It's very uncomfortable. Just ask right away: "I'm sorry, can you tell me your name again?" That's it.

Then write the name down. Use a memory trick, like visualization, to make it stick. Visualization goes a long way to help you remember information. If you can attach the person's name to something you can visualize—the crazier the better—it's going to help you remember. Say you're met a Mr. Hardy. How would you remember Mr. Hardy's name? You might connect him with the Hardee's fast-food chain. Or you could associate him with the classic comedy team Laurel and Hardy: you could picture this man walking around like Oliver Hardy.

Whatever works for you—the crazier, the better. If you meet somebody for the first time whose name is Ray, even if you can't remember their last name, attach something to the first name. Maybe you're picturing them with cool Ray-Ban sunglasses. Or you could imagine a ray of sunshine beaming down on that person; that will help remember that their name is Ray.

How about Carol? You might picture this person singing Christmas carols in a choir. Or if you remember the old *Carol Burnett Show*, she would tug her ear at the end of each episode, so you could picture Carol tugging at her ear. Again, the crazier you can make it, the better.

How about something a little tougher? How about Mrs. Jankowski? I might break it down into smaller chunks. I might picture a school janitor riding a cow on a pair of skis: *jan-cow-ski*. Think of a janitor riding a cow on skis. If you remember part of it, it'll get you to the rest.

How about this one? This happens quite frequently. You're at a business function and someone wants to introduce you to their coworkers: "Hey, these are my coworkers. This is Mary and Susan and Steve and Mike and Tim and Mark." Why can't you remember anybody's name here? You didn't have time to take the word association from short-term memory to long-term memory. You need a couple of seconds to make the transfer, but they've made the introductions too fast.

Here's one solution: say your contact is introducing you to five or six of their coworkers. As soon as they start—"Hey, these are my coworkers; this is Mark right here"—you jump in and move forward. Put your hand out to shake, make eye contact, and say your own name, then: "Hi, Mark. Nice to meet you." Here's the second person, Susan. "Hi, Susan. Nice to meet you also. " Here's the third person. Again: eye contact, handshake. "Hi, Mary, it's nice to meet you."

You're slowing your contact down. As soon as they introduce you to the first person, you jump in and shake the new person's hand. Now you have the few seconds you need to make the visual association. If you are introduced to five people and you can remember three of their names, it's a start.

Here's another situation. You're at a business function and you're talking to one of your colleagues. Obviously you know your colleague, but someone comes walking towards you, using your name and saying, "Hey, how are you? Good to see you again." You're thinking, "Who is this person? What am I going to do now? I'm probably going to have to introduce them to my colleague right here. I can't remember their name, but they sure remember mine."

This is a very embarrassing situation. There are a couple of common reactions. First, you avoid introducing anybody, and hopefully it'll be a short conversation. Probably not going to happen.

Maybe you could introduce your colleague, Mary, and say something like. "Hey this is my colleague, Mary, and this is . . ." This is awkward and embarrassing.

Here's a technique that works quite often—although not always. You're talking to a colleague. Here comes a person whose name you don't remember. When they're walking towards you, you greet this unknown person with some enthusiasm. You can shake their hand and say, "Hey, it's good to see you again. Have you had a chance to meet my colleague, Mary?" Lightly guide the unknown person's hand towards your colleague and step back a little. With that situation, there's a good chance that they're going to step up and say, "No, I have not. My name is such and such." Now you're out of it. Normally we introduce the person we know first, and then we're stuck with person number two, whose name we don't remember. In that case, start with the person you *don't* know. If it works 50 percent of the time, it's not a bad average.

Using Body Language

It's also a good idea to be aware of low power poses when you're communicating with people: in standing positions, low power positions are legs crossed, hiding your hands, and looking down. A low power pose in a seated position is looking away or down, with crossed arms, or leaning forward, looking dejected. Some people cross their arms because they're comfortable; they're not being defensive. Still, they can leave an impression of defensiveness and being closed off. Make a conscious effort to keep your arms down and open, and your hands open.

> Avoid low power positions, such as legs crossed; hiding your hands; crossed arms; leaning forward; and looking dejected.

If you go on a job interview, many companies will get feedback from the receptionist. When you sit down in the lobby, the receptionist is watching you as an applicant. What do you look like when you sit? Are you bored to death? Are you just going through the motions? Are you excited to be there? When you're in a public forum, people are watching all the time.

Power poses: open hands and open arms, looking forward, leaning forward, with hands on the hips. Also use a wider stance as opposed to crossed legs. Another possibility is to have arms crossed a little, but with a wider stance.

Another subtle gesture to look for: steepling your hands: your elbows are on the desk, your forearms are raised, your palms are separate, but your fingertips are touching, so that your hands are in a kind of steeple shape. Generally, this gesture shows confidence and possible connection. That usually means you're moving in the right direction: the other person is receptive to you and what you're proposing.

Another gesture to look for: someone may be telling you, "Oh yeah, I understand," but their eyes are partly closed. That means they *don't* understand. When people are confused, they will squint their eyes a little, so that their nose wrinkles. They're saying, "I'm trying hard to see this, but I just don't understand." Similarly, when people tilt their head slightly, they're trying to look at the question from a different angle, showing some confusion. If you see squinted eyes, with a bit of a head tilt when you are making an important point, you might want to back up and make your point again.

Here's a very subtle gesture. When you see somebody tugging at their ear or their eyeglasses during an important part of the conversation, it often means that they want to ask a question; they want to participate in the conversation. This goes back to childhood days. As kids in school, we were taught to raise our hands when we had a question. Adults have never really gotten out of that habit, but they're much better at hiding it. They'll do things like grabbing their ears or eyeglasses. It's as if they're saying, "I should be raising my hand, but I don't want to do it all the way."

When you see gestures like these, you may want to back up and let the other person participate and ask a question that they might have.

Workspace Decor

Now let's address some of the dos and don'ts of workspace decor. Obviously if you're at a company office, you want to follow company policies about what you can and what you can't have in your workspace. Always follow company policies.

If you're working at home, if there's really no policy written up, use common sense. Don't have anything in the background that could be seen as offensive or cause some kind of conflict. It might be a calendar with pictures that some people might consider to be offensive, or political items. The individual may be your candidate, but other people may not see it your way.

If you're working in an office with an open floor plan, avoid using air fresheners, especially if coworkers are nearby. You may have great intentions, but you may be offending somebody who has allergies. Don't be listening to music, videos, or podcasts out loud. Wear earphones.

Don't have sweets or candy at your desk, especially if you're trying to eat healthy, but also if you don't want a lot of drop-by visitors. Coworkers will always want to come by for the candy, and they'll want to chat a little.

A couple of dos, which are pretty self-explanatory: Decorate your workspace with items that make you feel good and comfortable—maybe plants, memorabilia, trophies, awards, books, motivational posters. If you like, you might have some personal items, such as photos of family or vacations or fishing trips. These things make you feel good. When you're tired and work is stressful, you can look at the photos and say, "This is what's really important in my life. This is why I go to work every day."

> Decorate your workspace with items that make you feel good.

Finally, here's an important point, and it's true even if you're self-employed and just starting out with not much money. Invest in a good chair with great support. If you're sitting for long periods of time when you work, you have to invest in a good chair, one that is adjustable and has good lumbar support. You can skimp on other things, but a good chair is like a pair of good shoes: you're going to use it all day, every day.

Summary

In this chapter, we've discussed how to make superior first impressions and add credibility when you're talking to your boss, colleagues, and customers. We've gone into how to craft a clear verbal message, and we went on to explore recovering from faux pas, the unspoken rules of business etiquette, the basic skills of networking, and giving productive criticism and feedback. The chapter also gave some important tips for reading faces and finding subtle clues to what someone is really saying beyond their words. Finally, it addressed some of the dos and don'ts of the workspace.

TWO

Enhancing Emotional Intelligence

This chapter will discuss emotional intelligence (EQ) and how to enhance it.

We'll start with an overview of what emotional intelligence is and why it's important. Then we'll proceed to elements of emotional intelligence that are related to self-awareness and self-management. The third section reviews EQ in relationships and task management. Then we'll turn to EQ as related to social awareness and impact. Finally, we'll look at ways to develop action plans that can enhance your emotional intelligence.

What Is Emotional Intelligence?

So what is emotional intelligence? It is your ability to recognize and manage your own emotions, recognize and respond to the emotions of others, build effective social relationships, and ultimately support your success at both work and home.

Often when people first hear the term *EQ* for *emotional intelligence*, they immediately think of IQ, which stands for *intelligence quotient*. In fact, emotional intelligence experts selected the abbreviation *EQ* to highlight that comparison. They wanted to make the point that EQ is often more important for professional success than IQ. Drawing that parallel helped them make that point.

Your IQ or intelligence quotient is generally understood to reflect your innate intelligence. It is generally measured early in life. You no doubt took tests in high school to help determine your IQ. Some researchers believe that IQ peaks in your late teens and early twenties. Once your IQ has been established, it's assumed to be fixed and stay quite stable over time, unless something dramatic happens.

EQ, on the other hand, can be developed over time. It's not just one measure but consists of many elements that we will review in this chapter. Unlike with IQ, high levels of EQ in any particular area may not be beneficial. For example, many people think of self-confidence as a positive trait. However, when self-confidence is taken too far—when we appear too self-confident to others—we may come across as arrogant.

EQ is often more important for professional success than IQ.

There are many benefits from developing your EQ. It can increase your productivity and job satisfaction. It can help you affect the perceptions of people around you and build interpersonal relationships. Understanding emotional intelligence helps us assess the fit between what we intended to do and the impact we have actually had. Many of our negative interactions with others occur when our intent does not match our impact. Developing emotional intelligence helps us close this gap.

Let's take a look at three different case studies. Often case studies will involve a caricature of someone who is always strict and harsh or someone who's always a pushover. The reality is much more complex, so let's look at three very different people.

First, there's Hank. Hank is always calm. Nothing seems to bother him, always even in his emotions and seemingly unflappable; happy Hank consistently shows a positive attitude. He always seems to see the bright side. While his team loves his positivity, there is a downside. Sometimes he seems a bit out of touch with the realities of what's going on, and his team tends to be afraid to bring him bad news: because he's such a positive guy, no one wants to disappoint him. As we review the different elements of emotional intelligence, think about which ones Hank may be under- and overusing.

Now meet Sherry. Sherry is a top performer and overachiever. She has high expectations for her team, builds expertise, and rewards performance fairly: exactly what you want for a meritocracy. Sherry pushes the limits of what's possible and, more often than not, achieves outcomes people never imagined. Her team loves her energy, but again, there's a downside. For every success, the bar is raised to new heights, and her team finds that the constantly raised expectations are becoming draining. Again, as we review the different elements of emotional intelligence, think about where you see Sherry across them.

Finally, there's Mark. Mark is connected to his team and highly responsive to their needs. As events unfold, his emotions and behaviors change. He wears his heart on his sleeve, and everyone knows at any given moment where his emotions lie. The team loves his authenticity but also find that working with Mark is a bit of a moving target. They feel as if they need to walk on eggshells because you never know what kind of mood he's going to be in. See if you observe Mark in the emotional elements that we will be reviewing.

Models of EQ

There are many different emotional intelligence models, and many authors have written about various elements and structures of EQ. Different authors see categories and group elements somewhat differently. There are trait-based emotional intelligence models and skills-based models. One philosophy approaches emotional intelligence as if it were like IQ: primarily inborn. Another perspective approaches emotional intelligence from a more skills-based perspective, believing that anyone can develop the different elements with awareness and practice. Others who discuss emotional intelligence are more theory-based, focusing on the concepts, while others are more measurement-based, focusing on assessments and measuring improvements over time.

The point of view in this chapter works to integrate all of these perspectives into a holistic look at emotional intelligence. It allows for the presence of inborn traits, acknowledges the important lessons that come from experience, and encourages the development of skills that come through reflection and practices.

For our purposes, we can group the elements of emotional intelligence into three separate categories. Although they are a little different from other models, they share many common elements.

> **The Elements of Emotional Intelligence**
> 1. Self-awareness and self-management
> 2. Relationship and task management
> 3. Social awareness and impact

The first category is self-awareness and self-management, a focus on *me*. The second category is relationship and task management, a focus on *us*. The third category is social awareness and impact, a focus on the broader social world.

With this overview in place, let's review our objectives. Our goal is to list the different elements of emotional intelligence and recognize behaviors associated with well-developed EQ. We want to help you assess your own strengths and weaknesses according to specific EQ elements. We also want to recognize the downside of overplaying certain traits of emotional intelligence. As we've seen, for example, too much self-confidence can appear to be arrogance. Too much flexibility can look like a lack of conviction. Finally, we will help you identify specific actions you can take to develop the elements of EQ.

A Four-Step Model

Before we move into the elements themselves, let's review a four-step model for developing EQ.

1. It is vital to observe yourself. Self-awareness and self-management support this step.
2. It is important to observe others and how they're reacting to you at any given moment. Do you appear to be achieving the impact and outcomes that you intended?
3. If it appears that you're not having the impact that you want, it's time to assess what needs to change.
4. After analyzing what you need to alter, you adjust and respond to the changes you see in ourselves and others.

You then repeat this cycle.

> **Four Steps for Developing EQ**
> 1. Observe yourself.
> 2. Observe others and their reactions.
> 3. Assess what needs to change.
> 4. Alter and adjust your responses.

Developing emotional intelligence is never completed. It's a constant series of observations and calibrations which result in certain impacts and outcomes. Developing emotional intelligence is a lifelong project. Let's take a closer look at its different components.

Self-Awareness

The first set of EQ elements have to do with you and your relationship to yourself. We're going to walk through each of these elements individually, but here's an overview.

First, we'll talk about self-awareness, also known as self-assessment; then we'll talk about self-regard and confidence. Third, we'll cover self-regulation, also known as impulse control. Next, we'll cover self-actualization, which some models call *motivation*. Finally, we'll cover independence, assertiveness, and flexibility.

We begin with self-awareness, or self-assessment. Most models list this element first because much of emotional intelligence centers upon your ability to recognize your own emotions and feelings in real time. This is the ability to reflect upon what you are feeling as you are feeling it and understand how those feelings are affecting you and others. It all begins with knowing yourself and being able to recognize how you are reacting to a situation in real time.

What are some ways to develop self-awareness? Ask yourself how often you think about your own emotions—reflecting on how you're feeling inside. When you are in a meeting, can you sense when your shoulders are rising out of stress, when your breath is quickening, or when your heart is beating faster? Sometimes our physical reactions to situations signal how we're feeling. If you are developing your ability to read your own emotions, paying attention to your body can be a good first step.

Here's another action to try. Before you go into a meeting, ask yourself, "How do I feel, and how do I want to feel at the end of this meeting? Do I want to feel calm, do I want to feel excited, do I want to feel powerful?"

At the end of that meeting, notice how you're feeling. How do you feel? Did you accomplish the feeling that you intended? This may all sound very touchy-feely to people who aren't used to asking these questions, but we are talking about emotional intelligence, so we do get quickly into the touchy-feely, and there's nothing wrong with that.

Your self-regard, also called *confidence* in some models, is your ability to recognize and own your strengths and weaknesses and to have some level of comfort with both. This comfort allows you to engage in the world with reasonable confidence in your talents. The ability to be objective and pragmatic about your strengths and weaknesses and accept yourself for who you are is a core foundation of emotional intelligence. Sometimes we'll hear the phrase, "To know me is to love me." People with healthy self-regard know and accept themselves and are comfortable in their own skins. They don't feel the need to be somebody else when they're with other people.

> People with healthy self-regard know and accept themselves.

Self-regulation and impulse control have to do with your ability to understand your own reactions and moderate them as appropriate. Impulse control refers to your ability to resist the urge to act in a certain way. Sometimes it is best not to jump in when somebody has pushed your buttons and to control your emotions rather than expressing them.

Emotional expression is equally important. Much of emotional intelligence is balancing different elements so that you're exercising them at the right time and place. Too much impulse control, for example, may lead to repressing your emotions instead of letting people know that you're reacting to what they're saying. Over time, this can lead to resentment. Knowing when to hold back and when to express emotions is a great example of balancing two different elements of emotional intelligence.

Next, we turn to self-actualization, which some models refer to as *motivation*. Self-actualization relates to your ability to shape and realize your own vision, to know what you want and feel empowered to go after it. Self-actualization supports your ability to successfully pursue your own goals and underlies any desire to improve yourself. Often when we call someone *driven*, it relates to self-actualization—to people who know how to create a future and make it real for themselves. Self-actualization is closely linked to a sense of control and self-efficacy: the belief that you can control your own destiny. The downside, of course, is that we aren't always in control. People with extremely high self-actualization may feel disappointed when they find they cannot achieve their goals through no fault of their own.

Linked to self-actualization is independence. Independence is the ability to stand on your own and make your own decisions. It relates to your ability to direct your own activities and avoid depending on others to shape your feelings. Independence allows us to individually decide how we feel about the events that are unfolding. Just because somebody else is sad or angry does not mean that we need to be sad or angry. Being able to accurately judge your own emotions without the need to look to others to see how you should be feeling is one aspect of independence. Often those with a high personal drive are also independent, but this is not always the case: some people may have a lot of drive but still look to others to dictate how they feel at any given moment.

Assertiveness relates to your ability to express your feelings and thoughts, primarily around advocating your own views and vision without hurting other people. This is related to your ability to express emotions, but a central principle here is advocacy: comfort in advocating your own perspective in front of others. Above we talked about self-regard and confidence. This element can be quiet in some people, who can feel confident without feeling assertive.

That said, you can see how these different elements overlap or interplay. They each have a slightly different focal point, but together relate to your overall sense of self-awareness and your ability to manage yourself.

Finally, there's flexibility. Flexibility refers to your ability to change as a situation changes. As events unfold, are you able to adjust to them while maintaining your sense of self-worth and identity? Are you open to the ideas of others and willing to change your mind given new information?

Again, thinking about the relationship between these elements, we see a need to balance independence and flexibility. There's benefit to being independent in your thinking, but there's also benefit in being flexible so you can accommodate any changes needed to meet the situation. Continuously balancing these different elements, depending on what's needed at a given time and place, is the overarching goal of emotional intelligence. Can you see what's needed in the moment and balance different factors appropriately?

We've already seen some examples of what can happen when a particular element is overdone or underdone. In general, overdoing self-awareness and self-management can take on the negative quality of self-absorption, where you're so busy examining yourself that you're unable to be attentive to others. Too much self-awareness and self-management may make you appear out of touch or disconnected from others. In short, too much all about *you* distracts from your ability to engage with others. The end result here can be a bit of a me-first orientation, where the needs of self get in the way of the needs of others.

On the other hand, too little self-awareness and self-management can be associated with a lack of ability to stand on one's own. People in this situation often seem to need someone else to feel fulfilled or even to know how they themselves are feeling at any given time. These individuals may benefit from developing self-awareness and self-management. If you find yourself unable to recognize and understand your own responses in different situations, these may be some areas you want to work on.

Here's a summary of key elements associated with self-awareness and self-management.

1. Know yourself.
2. Learn to be your own best friend. Humans are fundamentally social, so we're drawn to others, but the ability

to be by yourself without feeling lonely is a critical sign of well-developed emotional intelligence.
3. Another key principle is the ability to maintain your own identity, to know who you are, even when you are with a significant other or many people. You are the center of your own world. Self-awareness and self-management enable you to have a strong sense of core identity while being able to come into other people's worlds and engage productively.

Keys to Self-Management
1. Know yourself.
2. Learn to be your best friend.
3. Maintain your identity in all circumstances.

Relationship and Task Management

Now we can turn to relationship and task management. This set of EQ elements transitions out of the world of *me* and turns more to *us*: how we relate to other people and engage with them in the projects around us. These elements include empathy, emotional expression, interpersonal relationships, conflict management, reality testing, problem-solving, and teamwork and collaboration.

The elements of emotional intelligence are never purely independent. Just as with self-awareness and self-management, many of these elements closely relate to one another. When deployed effectively, they interact with and balance each other. Sometimes activating one element means deemphasizing another. This involves accurately reading what's happening around you and being sufficiently flexible to adjust your approach accordingly.

Let's start with empathy. We've already discussed the importance of recognizing your own emotions. Empathy relates to accurately detecting the emotions of others and recognizing how someone else might be feeling in any given moment. Empathy includes the ability to see another person's perspective and walk in their shoes. When we don't have enough empathy, we fail to recognize that someone else is reacting poorly to what's happening, that they're angry or sad or hurt. Now recognizing the emotions of others does not mean we have to take them on as our own. We must balance empathy with independence. This means recognizing what's happening to oneself while understanding what someone else is feeling. While you may change your behavior accordingly, you don't take on someone else's emotions as you own. Too much empathy can lead to projection: you take on emotions because you see them in another.

Balance empathy with independence.

If you sense that you need to develop empathy but you're not quite sure how to read someone else's feelings, you can start by asking them, "I'm having a hard time reading you right now. How are you feeling about what I'm saying?" If that seems too touchy-feely to you, simply ask, "What are your thoughts on all this?" Then wait for an answer. Even if the response is not presented in emotionally oriented words, you should get a sense of how the person is feeling by what they express to you.

Emotional Expression

Emotional expression is the ability to appropriately express and share your own feelings. We've already talked about being aware of your own emotions. Emotional expression relates to your ability to appropriately express those emotions with others. This includes both verbal communication and body language.

Emotional expression both balances and complements impulse control. You need to decide at any given moment whether it's more appropriate to hold back your emotions (feeling but not showing them) or to let others know how you're feeling at this particular time.

Say a particular manager tends to hold back on showing anger. She errs on the side of soothing and understanding and recognizing where she is at fault in any particular situation, with a philosophy that the only person she can truly control is herself.

However, sometimes an employee pushes the manager too hard. That person is showing enough patterns of behavior that the manager can reasonably conclude that this person needs to adjust, because the manager is not resolving the issue by adjusting her own. In those cases, sometimes she chooses to show irritation and frustration. It doesn't happen very often, so usually this does lead to a significant change from the other person. The manager may ask herself, "Had I shown my frustration earlier, could we have avoided reaching this point?"

Sometimes the answer is yes. Developing emotional intelligence is a constant process of reflection and recalibration while recognizing which elements are harder for you and which come more easily.

Interpersonal relationships involve the ability to build and maintain relationships with others, and, once we have these relationships, to find satisfaction in them and to be generally happy with them. For some people this can mean having very few close friends. For others, it may mean having a broad set of friends and relying on different people for different needs. The question is not how many interpersonal relationships you have or how deep they are on some kind of scale. The question is, do you have relationships that are satisfying for you?

Part of any relationship is managing conflict. This includes the ability to recognize that a conflict is happening, determine what might be causing it, and separate out the actual problems from the people involved. This does not mean objectifying every conflict such that people aren't important. It's simply about recognizing what is task-based versus what is relationship-based in any particular conflict.

Managing Conflict

- Recognize that a conflict is happening.
- Determine the cause.
- Separate out the actual problems from the people involved.

When conflict management is well-developed, we're able to use conflict productively to advance a project or a relationship to the next level. People tend to only enter into conflict for the things that are important to them, so when somebody's engaged in conflict, it gives you unique insight into what's important to them. Learning about that value helps you build a relationship with the other person.

Reality Testing

Reality testing is the ability to perceive facts accurately and objectively see things for what they are. Have you ever heard someone accused of only wearing rose-colored glasses or always seeing the glasses as half empty even when things are going reasonably well? People with well-developed reality testing are willing to ask questions that test their hypotheses or hunches. If I tend to assume that everything's going great, am I willing to ask the tough questions that will reveal a different underlying truth? If I tend to assume things are not going to go well, am I willing to ask questions that allow me to see what's actually working?

This quality can seem closely related to optimism and pessimism, and indeed it is. Reality testing helps us assess the accuracy of our level of optimism or pessimism. If you're not sure how to assess your level of reality testing, ask yourself some questions:

- Am I seeing this situation at face value, or am I projecting other experiences onto this situation that may make my perceptions less accurate?

- Am I making certain assumptions that may not be true in this situation?
- What questions could I ask to test those assumptions?

Reality testing is about whether you're allowing your emotions to cloud your perceptions. Are you able to separate out those emotions in order to have a more objective, problem-centered view? On the other hand, people who overemphasize reality testing may miss the emotional context of a situation. The importance of facts does change based on the people involved. Objectively evaluating both facts and context are important facets of reality testing.

Next is problem-solving. At first, this appears to be more closely related to cognitive functioning than to emotional intelligence. In this case, however, we are focusing on your ability to gather information and analyze and solve problems—but through the lens of the emotions. How are yours and others' emotions impacting the problem at hand? How can you use those emotions to lead to better outcomes? For example, can you harness the frustration of others in order to solve a shared problem? If you are engaged in a change management project, can you detect the level of anxiety in others about the change? Can you adjust the plan in order to lower anxiety while encouraging incremental success that will demonstrate that the change will be a positive one? If you're a project manager, you're going to need a full array of emotional intelligence elements to solve problems.

Teamwork and collaboration in outcomes relate to an overall ability to work well with others in a group situation and synthesize their views to create the best outcomes. Of course, this quality is supported by interpersonal relationships, reality testing, and problem-solving. Nevertheless, the ability to engage in a group is somewhat different than the ability to engage in one-on-one settings. It takes advanced emotional intelligence to deal with the emotions of many people working towards a shared goal in a single time and place. The skills of group facilitation and team building directly flow from this element of emotional intelligence.

Let's take a look at what happens when you either overemphasize or underemphasize relationship and task management. Too much emphasis on relationships and task management can lead to too much attention on people's emotions. It may lead you to be overly involved in the affairs and work of others or to rely excessively on them. If you've received feedback that you are needy or that you struggle with working on your own, you may be overdoing this set of emotional intelligence elements.

In contrast, relationships and task management can also be comparatively neglected, leading to a lack of connection with others, isolation, loneliness, or an inability to work with others to achieve individual and group goals. One sign of this deficiency may be reacting to a group project by thinking, "I could have done this much faster on my own." Excessive self-actualization and independence can indicate that you're underemphasizing relationships.

To sum up, we need to be able to read others, anticipate their needs, build bridges with them, and come out on those bridges to connect and collaborate. I may begin with *me*, but I must extend to *us* in a comfortable and productive way.

Social Awareness and Impact

The final set of emotional intelligence elements that we'll explore has to do with the social world. Humans are designed to be social. When we enter into the world as babies, we are completely dependent on other people for several years. For our very survival, we must connect with others, rely on them, and give of ourselves in an interactive and mutually beneficial way. In our social structure, no one is able to completely survive on their own. In fact, this biological reality largely drives the need for emotional intelligence.

So this final set of elements relates to social awareness and impact: your impact on your world and the impact of the world on you. Elements covered here are developing others, organizational and community awareness, social responsibility and service orientation, optimism, happiness, and stress tolerance.

Elements of Social Awareness
- Developing others
- Organizational and community awareness
- Social responsibility
- Service orientation
- Optimism
- Happiness
- Stress tolerance

Developing others relies on relationship and task management, but focuses these elements on helping others. Are you able to recognize the growth opportunities in others and support their learning? To assess your level of emotional intelligence at this element, consider the ten people you work most closely with. Do you have a general sense of their strengths and weaknesses, and could you come up with a list of development actions from which you think they would benefit? If you're able to do that, to what degree have you acted on that knowledge? Have you shown someone how to do something that they would clearly benefit from knowing? Have you had the courage to provide someone with needed and constructive feedback so they can achieve more effective outcomes?

Many managers report that giving feedback to others is an activity that scares them the most and that they do the least often. This leads to a general discomfort about matters such as performance appraisals. If we think about performance appraisals as opportunities to develop others and increase their happiness, self-actualization, and problem-solving, it may become a little bit easier.

Organizational and community awareness relates to your awareness of the collective emotions and culture of your organization and community. What's the general tone of your workplace, and how do you moderate your interactions with others based on that tone? Is your workplace one that's more traditional and process-oriented, where respect for the rules and preexisting ways of doing things is highly valued? Or does your workplace value excitement and change, constant innovation, and looking for new opportunities? How you engage with people in these two different workplaces may differ, depending on whether you're trying to support the status quo or change it.

Social savvy also includes the ability to read the larger political field, to know who's truly in charge regardless of the organizational chart, and to know how to move around this world for better outcomes. Many write off organizational politics as undesirable and best avoided. However, part of effective reality testing is understanding how the workplace works, and part of problem-solving is being able to maneuver within it.

The next element is social responsibility or service orientation. This has to do with an overarching sense of responsibility as well as a need and willingness to serve others. Here are some good questions to assess your level of emotional intelligence in this arena:

- How often do you volunteer?
- Does it occur to you to volunteer?
- How do you support your neighborhood or community?
- In a bad storm or other emergency, how quickly would it occur to you to look in on a neighbor?
- Do you even know your neighbors?
- Are you active in your community association, local government, or some other social organization?

Not everyone chooses to serve in a public way. Serving others can happen more privately and personally. The question is, how often do you feel this sense of responsibility, and how often do you tend to act on it?

We can close with three elements that highlight your personal interaction with your social world. The first is an overarching sense of optimism: the ability to remain hopeful about the future and to be resilient in the face of disappointment. Do you believe things will turn out well even if the results weren't exactly what you had planned? Do you generally believe that you'll be able to face the challenges that may emerge in the future?

Optimism relates closely to both reality testing and self-actualization. Despite the reality that faces you, do you have a high enough level of self-actualization that you believe you'll be able to shape your world and those outcomes will generally be positive?

One way to develop a sense of optimism is to reflect on past events where the outcome could have been bad but ended up being just fine, then to apply that insight to a situation about which you're feeling negative right now. What possible outcomes could be just as good as what you most hope for, even in light of all the bad things that could happen? Apply some reality testing to assess the probability that bad outcomes will actually occur. If you truly believe a bad outcome is likely, exercise your self-actualization to determine what problem-solving steps you could take to adjust that outcome. Here we blend multiple emotional intelligence elements to enhance an overall sense of optimism.

> One way to develop a sense of optimism is to reflect on past events where the outcome could have been bad but ended up being just fine.

Happiness is another overarching element of emotional intelligence. It's an emergent element, which relates to your general sense of well-being and satisfaction with the world and your life. It is hard to affect happiness directly, but it tends to increase when you develop all the other elements of emotional intelligence so that you're adjusting your reactions and responses to the needs of a situation or the people involved.

Assessing your level of happiness is as simple as periodically pausing and asking yourself, "Am I happy?" If you're not sure, developing self-awareness may help you answer the question. If the answer is, "I think I could be happier," think about the present obstacles to your happiness and the elements of emotional intelligence you could use to move in a more positive direction. Are you lacking in self-confidence? Do you feel lonely? Would you benefit from developing more relationships with others? Are you lacking a sense of overarching meaning and impact, which you might develop by helping others? Do you consistently feel anxiety or a lack of control, which may be helped by an increased sense of confidence, assertiveness, or independence? Emotional intelligence provides the framework to ask these kinds of questions.

Speaking of anxiety or a sense that you aren't in control, let's turn to the final element covered here, which is stress tolerance. This element relates to your ability to process and cope with stressful situations and bounce back from disappointment. Your ability to accommodate and manage stress affects your ability to control the other facets of emotional intelligence in the moment. It also directly affects your overall sense of optimism and happiness. Do you consistently feel your shoulders hunched, your heart beating quickly, or a general sense of anxiety when something goes wrong? Do you react in a way that prevents you from making the best choices at that time? If so, stress tolerance and relaxation techniques may be an area to focus on.

> Stress tolerance relates to your ability to process and cope with stressful situations and bounce back from disappointment.

When we overdo social awareness, we may experience too much emphasis on giving without getting anything back or attending to our own needs. Our level of stress may become unhealthy if we're spending too much time focusing on service to others and not enough time on self. An overemphasis on these elements can make you appear overly subordinate or subservient. Overcommitting can also reduce your results because you're too scattered across too many activities. On the other hand, when social awareness is underdeveloped, you may feel a lack of a larger connection to the social structures around you. A lack of awareness of the world around you can also hinder your effectiveness and make you appear out of touch.

Key principles associated with social awareness and impact are the abilities to contribute to society and give without getting. Remember that humans are fundamentally social and that you are truly part of something larger than yourself. Developing these emotional intelligence elements can help you both contribute to and benefit from this larger *something*.

Action Planning and Next Steps

Thinking about all the different emotional intelligence elements and how they balance or conflict with each other can seem overwhelming. Why should we engage in this process?

Well-developed emotional intelligence increases resiliency and productivity as well as the ability to get yourself unstuck when in a less than positive situation. Developing relationship and task management leads to more effective communication and better and deeper relationships that you can draw upon when things get difficult or problems emerge. Well-developed emotional intelligence also leads to greater connection with a social world and a greater sense of peace.

So how do we get there? Let's review the four-step model introduced at the beginning of this chapter:

1. We must observe ourselves. We need to know how we're feeling at any given moment and what actions we might need to take as a result.
2. We need to consistently observe others in order to assess how they're feeling and how they're reacting to what we're doing.
3. Based on our observations of self and others, we need to assess the needs for better outcomes at this moment.
4. We adjust and respond based on this analysis.

After making a change, we begin the cycle all over again with observing ourselves and others. What was the change we wanted to see, and what do we need to adjust as a result?

Exercising emotional intelligence means repeating the cycle over and over again every day. You engage in many activities without really thinking about it because you're so used to doing them. You can do the same with this model if you apply it consistently.

Back to Hank, Sherry, and Mark

Now that we have a vocabulary of emotional intelligence, let's return to our original three case studies: Hank, Sherry, and Mark.

First, let's revisit unflappable, happy Hank. We love Hank's positivity, but he seems a little out of touch. What can Hank do? First, he needs to be aware of, and accept, that a problem even exists. We hope that Hank has both self-awareness and the interpersonal relationships that enable him to seek feedback and reflect upon himself. In order to change, Hank needs to be more aware of himself and his impact on others.

Let's assume that he is aware of both the positive and negative impacts he's having, has a strong enough sense of self- regard that he accepts himself for who he is, but is willing to change to increase his effectiveness.

Given that, what can Hank do? He might benefit from increased reality testing. His high sense of optimism and seeing the bright side is positive, but asking some tough questions so he's accurately assessing the facts and their impact may lead his team to be more confident that he understands the complexities involved. Hank may also benefit from increasing his range of emotional expression. If the world only sees happiness from him, but internally he's feeling quite frustrated, he may benefit from showing some of that emotion to others. This way, others will understand that he gets it, and Hank may be better able to effect the change that internally he wants to see.

Now let's revisit high-standard Sherry. We love Sherry's energy, but her demands are draining. The team is achieving great things, yet it never seems good enough.

Let's assume that Sherry holds not only others but herself to a high standard and is willing to acknowledge and adjust her behavior for better outcomes.

Sherry may benefit from decreasing her assertiveness and self-actualization and increasing her emphasis on interpersonal relationships and empathy. Sherry needs to be sensitive to the line between motivation and futility. Many people benefit from, and even want to be challenged and pushed. When you challenge me, you demonstrate your faith in my abilities, and that's very motivating. But when challenged in excess, I feel that anything I do is never going to be quite good enough; at that point, a switch is flipped and my motivation may disappear. Sherry needs to be able to read the individual members of her team well enough to know where that line is for them and navigate it well. This requires a tremendous amount of sensitivity and an ability to read others.

Let's turn to moving-target Mark. Mark wears his heart on his sleeve. You always know what he's feeling. We love his authenticity, but we tend to be at the edge of our seats, never knowing how he will react to something. Mark is engaging in emotional expression but may benefit from some impulse control. We don't want him to fully hide his feelings, because we love his authenticity, but Mark needs to remember to balance his own needs with those of others and balance his expression accordingly.

Is Mark aware of the range of emotions he's feeling through the course of a day with his team? We tend to assume that people who show a lot of emotions understand their own emotions. That's not always true. In this case, it would be valuable to learn about how he perceives his own emotions and how much he's aware of expressing them to others.

To get started in using the model, it's important to establish a baseline. Take some time to reflect on recent experiences, what went well and what you wish you had handled differently. Many people benefit from completing emotional intelligence self-assessments or skills tests to get a snapshot of their own internal world. While it can be hard to hear, requesting feedback from others is a powerful way to develop your emotional intelligence (if you're willing to engage in the process). You can complete a 360 assessment, also known as 360-degree feedback, which is a performance review method that involves getting formal feedback from people that report to you, from your peers, and from your boss.

> Requesting feedback from others is a powerful way to develop your emotional intelligence.

You also can ask for informal feedback from people who know you well. Your might say, "I'm interested in your thoughts on how that project went." Let them talk about the project a bit, and then gently ask if they have any advice on how you could change your approach on future projects. This is a nonthreatening way to get some feedback, because you're asking in the context of a project, not of you personally.

Then you can interpret what the others say through the framework of emotional intelligence. You can test your hypothesis by saying, "It sounds like I might benefit from . . ." Fill in the blank, such as: "getting to know my team better," "better assessing the reality of the situation," or "being more assertive." The other person can then either validate those proposals or clarify what they meant.

Finally, think about patterns of feedback you've gotten over time. Often as we change jobs and move through life, we hear similar themes in our feedback. As previously mentioned, we have inborn traits that may be solidified or moderated by lessons from experience, and we can shape those traits through skills development. Recognizing the patterns that have followed us through time and recognizing why we are the way we are supports our self-regard. It can also point to changes that may take a lifetime to develop.

Here are some practical questions for applying this model and developing your own action plan. Consider times when your impact didn't match your intent. What could you do differently next time? Think about the impact you want to have in a coming conversation or meeting. How do you plan to engage in that interaction to increase the chance that you're going to have the impact that you want? What small adjustment do you want to make for any emotional intelligence element? What is the desired benefit of changing? What small action are you willing to do in the hope that it will yield better outcomes?

Let's bring these ideas together to apply the four-step model. First, you may observe yourself. You may think, "I feel stressed during team meetings when there's not enough time, and I know I don't manage that stress well. I observe others when I'm stressed. They appear more stressed and just stop talking and shut down."

Now adjust the needs based on those observations: "I need to either lengthen my meetings or better manage my stress with others so I adjust and respond. I lengthen the meeting, and I actively smile and adjust my body."

As a result, say that the next meeting went better, but the energy was lower, and participants seemed to wander a bit.

You tell yourself, "I acknowledged I was feeling stressed. I made some changes and a different outcome occurred. Now I need to rebalance again and use some assertiveness to keep the energy high, but without reintroducing the stress."

Again, this model is a constant process of recalibration and adjustment. As we've stressed, developing emotional intelligence is an ongoing process. You are never done. Moreover, unlike IQ, emotional intelligence is not just about you. It's about other people and the context. What is needed in some situations may not work in others. Well-developed emotional intelligence requires constant recalibration.

If you're interested in learning more about emotional intelligence models and elements, here are some great references. Daniel Goleman, known as the father of emotional intelligence, has written a number of popular books on the subject: the first, *Emotional Intelligence: Why It Can Matter More than EQ*, published in 1995, brought the subject to widespread attention.

The EQ Edge: Emotional Intelligence and Your Success, by Steven E. Stein and Howard R. Book, is a resource describing one of the more popular emotional intelligence models. Hile Rutledge translated many of these ideas into a great workbook called *The EQ Workbook*, which focuses on action planning. Finally, if you're interested in an assessment, Reuven Bar-On's Bar-On Model of Emotional-Social Intelligence is a good option.

Summary

Let's review what we've covered in this chapter. We began by providing an overview of emotional intelligence and its importance. Next, we reviewed many emotional intelligence elements, focusing on self-awareness and management, relationship and task management, and social awareness and impact. Finally, we closed with a discussion of action planning and next steps.

This chapter has hopefully provided you with a framework for thinking about emotional intelligence as well as a practical sense of what you can do to develop it.

THREE

Active Listening Skills

We'll now turn to active listening skills to improve communication. In this chapter, you will learn what active listening is; eliminate barriers to active listening; the six steps for active listening; how to deliver effective feedback using interactive listening; and creating connection through active listening.

What Is Active Listening?

Active listening is a skill for building rapport and understanding with others by listening beyond someone else's words to understand the total meaning of what they are saying. Active listening is a proven technique for building trust and resolving conflict by helping others to communicate freely. It aims to bring about change. This can be a change in relationships, attitudes, and even behaviors in both the speaker and the listener.

> Active listening is the skill of listening beyond someone else's words to understand the total meaning of what they are saying.

These changes do not come about from advising, trying to fix others, or telling them what they should have done. Rather, change results because the active listener is employing specific techniques that demonstrate sensitivity and create a safe space for the speaker to articulate exactly what he or she means and feels.

Have you ever had a conversation where you've said to someone else, "You aren't listening to me," and they respond, "I heard you"? Listening and hearing are not the same thing. We listen, yet we do not hear. Often when we listen, we hear the words, pass them through our own filter, assign an interpretation from our own point of view, and often end up with a meaning that is not at all what the speaker intended.

Communication is the number one life skill. Active listening is the foundation of that skill. To be an active listener, you will have to employ the fifth habit in Stephen R. Covey's *Seven Habits of Highly Effective People*: "Seek first to understand and then to be understood." This is a complete shift in mindset: shifting from getting your point across to listening in order to understand the actual meaning of the other person's words.

Most of the frustration, relationship breakdowns, inefficiencies, and conflict we have experienced with other people have resulted from the absence of the skill of effective communication—specifically, the absence of the core foundation of this skill, which is active listening.

> "Seek first to understand, and only then to be understood." —*Stephen R. Covey*

As you prepare to begin using the specific techniques you will learn in this chapter, start by exercising Stephen Covey's fifth habit: in every conversation, seek first to understand and only then to be understood.

Why do we listen yet do not hear? If you are like most people, you want to get your point across in a conversation. You probably seek to be understood, but in so doing, you may end up completely ignoring the other person, only pretending that you're listening. Or your filter gets in the way, and you only hear some parts of the conversation, missing the major meaning completely.

Why does this happen? Most people listen with the intent to reply rather than to understand. As a result, they listen and formulate a response while the other person is speaking. You filter everything you hear through your own life experiences, your own frame of reference. This is called *autobiographical listening*. An autobiography is a person writing the story of their own life: in this case, we are listening through the stories of our own lives. We check what we hear against our own autobiography to see how it measures up, disconnecting from the actual meaning. When someone says, "You are not listening," they're really saying, "Your own story is in the way. You are not hearing the meaning of what I'm really saying." By contrast, when you listen, you seek to understand the real meaning of the other person's words.

To shift into active listening, ask yourself these questions in order to check your own filter.

- Do I focus on getting my point across during a conversation?
- Do I think about my reply as someone is speaking?
- How is my filter?
- Do I measure what other people are saying against my own experiences?
- Do I make up my mind before someone has finished speaking?

One woman used to start laughing during heated arguments with her husband. She could watch his body begin to rock back and forth, like a fighter getting ready to enter the ring. The wheels in his mind were turning: he was thinking about what he was going to say. The woman learned to laugh and pause and say, "I see you're doing it: you're formulating a response. I really just need you to listen and not think about your reply."

We all have these habits. Check your filter; move out of your story so you can hear the meaning of what the other person is saying.

Carl R. Rogers and Richard E. Farson formulated typical responses that result from autobiographical listening.

Evaluating is when you listen in order to judge and then either agree or disagree. The entire time someone else is speaking, you are listening with the intention of judging the content of their speech and determining whether or not you agree or disagree with what they're saying.

Probing is listening in order to ask questions from your own frame of reference. Sometimes *advising* follows probing. In this case, you respond immediately with advice. You are not actively listening to demonstrate empathy and acknowledge the other person's words and feelings so as to grasp their meaning and build connection.

Probing followed by advising can create a breakdown. When you listen for the purpose of advising and you respond by giving that advice, one of two things can result. In the first place, the other person might stop coming to you altogether because they wanted you to actively listen instead of giving them advice based on your own frame of reference.

In the second place, advising can create learned helplessness. The other person comes to you all the time; they never reflect by asking themselves critical questions or change behaviors. By constantly providing advice, you have created learned helplessness in the relationship, eliminating any possibility for change for the other person.

Then there's *interpreting*: listening to and analyzing the other person's motives and behaviors based upon your own experiences. Has your filter been getting in the way of understanding? Very frequently, what they're saying and how you interpret it are two completely different things.

Four Behavioral Styles

The key to moving out of autobiographical listening and into active listening is to use the Platinum Rule, created by Dr.

Anthony J. Alessandra, to encourage active listening. The Platinum Rule—which is a version of the Golden Rule—is to treat people the way they want to be treated. In your natural communication habits, are you treating people the way you want to be treated? How might your natural personality style be discouraging and thus create a breakdown in relationships? To encourage active listening, you must first learn to speak the language of the other person; otherwise, will they really be able to hear you?

In his book *Relationship Strategies: Using the Platinum Rule to Create Behavioral Rapport*, Dr. Alessandra describes four major behavioral styles, each of which displays an intent in communication. *Thinkers* intend to get it right. *Directors* intend to get it done. These two are called the *get it right people* and the *get it done people* respectively. These are task-based people. The other two types are the *relaters* and the *socializers*. Relaters want to get along, and socializers want to be appreciated.

Four Major Behavioral Styles
1. Thinkers: get it right
2. Directors: get it done
3. Relaters: get along
4. Socializers: get appreciated

You naturally approach listening from your own point of view and personality style, and you are passing information through that filter. Every behavioral style has both strengths and weaknesses in communicating. Consider which personality style fits you and which natural tendencies of that style might be barriers to active listening.

Since the thinker intends to get it right, the natural response for you if you are a thinker is to evaluate. You are listening through that filter, which always intends to get it right, so you listen for what's wrong. You are judging to determine if you agree or disagree with the speaker. If there are grammatical or factual errors in what they are saying, rather than removing those so that you can focus on deeper meaning, you may be completely distracted. If there are errors, you might even correct the person when you respond.

Thinkers listen in order to evaluate.

Thinkers tend to have lots of probing questions because you are a problem solver, which is a strength. But if you launch into specific types of probing questions that are passed through a filter, it can suggest to the speaker that you aren't listening for meaning and didn't really hear them. They may even shut down in response.

Directors intend to get it done, so you are listening for the purpose of solving the problem. If your natural personality style is that of a director, a get it done person, your response will most likely be to offer advice or a solution. You yourself wouldn't go to someone unless there was something you wanted them to do, so you tend to assume that if someone's speaking to you, they must want you to solve a problem or take some kind of action.

Directors listen in order to solve problems.

But listening is an action. Sometimes the only thing the other person wanted you to do was actively listen and indicate (through some of the techniques you will learn in this book) that you heard them.

Relaters intend to get along. If this is your style, you want to connect with others and their experiences, but you are often interpreting what they are saying through your own experience. You either make statements of sympathy—"I'm so sorry that happened to you"—or just let them go on and on, which is different from active listening. At this point, they're just dumping on you. As the relater, your natural tendency to sympathize is getting in the way of empathy, establishing deeper meaning, and creating change for both people.

Relaters listen in order to get along.

The socializer intends to be appreciated. If that's your natural style, you may be outgoing, fun, and communicative: you love people, you're a people person, and people may want to come to you. But as they tell you their story or their issue, your personality style may lead you to give unsolicited, maybe even off-topic advice. You may expand the initial discussion beyond the scope of what they intended, or you may interpret, pass their information through your filter, and begin to tell your own story about a similar situation. You do this with the best of intentions, thinking it will show them that you have listened and can relate. But giving too many examples from your own experience can be a turnoff, create disconnection, and drive people away.

> Listeners listen in order to be appreciated.

We all have a natural personality style, and the weaknesses of our style can discourage others from talking freely, particularly with opposite types. Determine your natural personality style, and understand its strengths and weaknesses. That way, you'll be able to use the Platinum Rule to meet people where they are and treat them as they want to be treated.

Eliminating Barriers to Active Listening

Here are some statements that you can use in your own internal dialogue to open yourself up to actively listening.

- What others feel is important.
- I respect others even though I may not agree.
- I release the need to change or evaluate others.
- I want to be the kind of person others can talk to.

The internal scripts that we all have start running immediately, interfering with our ability to hear the meaning behind what someone else is saying. Internal messages like those above will help you shift your attitudes.

Once you've shifted your attitude through internal dialogue, it's important to eliminate any possible barriers to listening actively and employ the techniques you will be learning. Your interest level in the speaker or the subject can interfere; so can interruptions, whether they come from your own natural tendency to interrupt or from outside. In a fast-paced world, where we often think we can multitask, we are really not present in the moment. Think about how you can minimize interruptions, and stop your own tendency to interrupt.

Rehearsing responses is a common barrier. Listening autobiographically and formulating a response even as the person is speaking interferes with your ability to hear the deeper meaning. Similarly, distractions, whether they come from outside or from your internal thoughts, will keep you from being present and listening in the moment.

Questions are a major barrier to active listening. Think about what happens to you when you're trying to communicate to someone. As soon as you stop speaking, they launch into a series of *whys*: "Why were you thinking that?" *Why* sounds accusatory and will put the speaker on the defensive.

Preaching or moralizing is a major turnoff—coming from your own interpretation and advising someone from a place of judgment. This often results from evaluating: "Do I agree? Do I disagree?" Reserve judgment.

Active Listening Skills

Time is a natural barrier to active listening. You will have to create time in your day to practice it. (Later we'll talk about how to find optimum space during your day.) The moment your emotions are triggered, if you escalate, your logical response will be reduced biologically in the brain, interfering with your ability to employ the techniques of active listening.

Techniques for Mastering Your Emotions

These are some techniques that will help you be present and manage your emotions:

- Remove distractions, like email, checking texts, or rehearsing your response.
- Breathe. Breathing activates the logical center of the brain, and if you are breathing with your mouth, you won't be talking with it and interrupting someone else.
- Make eye contact. Fifty-five percent of communication is nonverbal. Eye contact demonstrates that you are present in the moment and actively engaging your senses to listen.
- Relax your jaw. Sometimes facial muscles make a person look tense, so be aware of your face. A relaxed jaw presents an open posture for listening.
- Silence all electronics.
- Identify your optimum time of day. We all have a time of day where we are more available mentally and physically for active listening.
- Do not dig to force a dialogue. Avoid digging beyond what someone is willing to share.

Set yourself up for success. What's your active listening plan? Stephen Covey says that one of the seven habits of highly effective people is that they begin with the end in mind. As you begin moving into active listening exercises, identify an accountability partner: someone who will work with you to practice the techniques. Choose low-risk subject matter at first: easy things you can talk about, anything from the weather to the basics of the day. Then set a timer for these conversations. Three- to five-minute conversations will allow you to practice with repetition. Keep track of what we call LB's and NT's: things that you *like best* and what you will do differently *next time,* so you are always sharpening the saw. Develop your plan and practice these techniques daily so that with repetition you can remove old patterns of responding ineffectively.

Successful people begin with the end in mind.

Steps to Active Listening

As one spiritual advisor says, listening has no judgment. Listening has no expectation. Most of all, listening is a process of love.

Here are six major steps for active listening. They will enable you to learn how to listen for meaning beyond the words of what someone is saying:

- Reflecting
- Encouraging

- Identifying emotions
- Validation
- Probing questions
- Using silence and pauses

Let's explore each one of these six steps.

Reflecting is paraphrasing and restating the feelings and words of the speaker. It indicates that you understand the meaning beyond the content.

You can use two different techniques for reflecting: *mirroring* and *paraphrasing*. Reflecting allows the speaker to hear their own thoughts and focus on what they say and feel. Sometimes when you exactly reflect back what you heard, the speaker is surprised to hear what really came out of their mouth. They will then adjust what they said or have a moment of self-reflection.

Reflecting also shows the speaker that you are really trying to experience the world as they see it. You are putting yourself in their shoes rather than listening autobiographically from your own experience. You are doing your best to understand the meaning of what they are saying.

You reflect first by mirroring, which is telling someone what they've said word for word. A classic example of mirroring: you go to a restaurant, order a cheeseburger with ketchup only, a small order of fries, and a small Coke. Mirroring back, the waiter says, "You ordered a cheeseburger with ketchup only, a small order of fries, and a small Coke. Did I get that right?"

If you're trying to build an immediate consensus on some factually based information, it might be best to mirror. Mirroring can be very effective when beginning to talk about difficult topics, because the person speaking can hear their own words. You'll often see this used in relationship counseling when clients begin talking about subjects that make them feel vulnerable.

> With mirroring, you simply repeat back what you've heard.

Mirroring completely removes judgment, because you're not even attempting to paraphrase; you're just repeating back what you heard. It starts to open up a safe space when you are in the beginning stages of learning about one another. But use this technique only occasionally, because if you use it too much, it can become annoying.

Paraphrasing takes the words plus feeling statements to indicate meaning. You move beyond the content to indicate what somebody really feels. A classic example of paraphrasing is a situation where an employee is talking to the manager about the bathroom and says, "I finally finished cleaning the disgusting restrooms." Instead of just focusing on the words, the manager focuses on feeling. The words "finally" and "disgusting" indicate that this employee might feel frustrated or stressed. The manager might paraphrase by saying, "I understand you completed the restrooms. Sounds like it was a bit of an unpleasant task."

To use reflecting in active listening, first observe the speaker's body language and verbal cues. Listen with as many of your senses as possible. Astute listeners are able to look beyond content to observe the other person's physical being. People communicate frustration, stress, anger, fear, guilt, and shame in the way they hold their bodies. Paying attention to nonverbal cues will quickly help you to accurately reflect content, plus emotion and the intensity of that emotion.

In the reflecting stage, do not add any additional content or elevate the vocabulary. Don't add higher-level words or correct someone else's grammar. When paraphrasing, keep it simple. Use this formula: you feel, plus an indication of intensity, plus an emotional word: "I *hear* that you *feel slightly frustrated* when a person gives you an assignment and then sends a follow-up email asking you where you are on that assignment." You have said *that* they feel, *what* they feel, and *how intensely* they feel it. Stating the emotion and the level of intensity is important to building connection and indicating your interest in the true meaning. This technique will allow you to hear what the other person is really saying and feeling. By reflecting, you are showing the speaker that you are trying to perceive the world and their experiences as they see them.

To encourage someone, use brief, positive verbal or nonverbal cues that lead them to continue. A simple head nod gives the verbal cue *yes* as someone is speaking. Follow up with expressions like, "Really!" "Did you?" and "Then what?" They will cue the speaker to continue. This is different from merely nodding or making extraneous noises—"Uh-huh, uh-huh"—while someone is speaking. These annoying habits are actually interruptions and can be perceived as trying to rush someone through their content.

Use eye contact; smile. Remember your facial expressions. You can have a thoughtful look on the face that indicates interest. Hold your body in a relaxed posture, with relaxed jaw, hands, neck, and shoulders. Be aware of your physical posture in the light of encouraging. Some people signal that they are not approachable without saying anything verbally: they're communicating entirely through body language. How is your body language? Are you encouraging as an active listener?

Validating others is an important step for active listening. To validate is to acknowledge the individual's problems, issues, and feelings—to listen openly and with empathy and respond in a way that demonstrates interest. For example, you might say, "I appreciate your willingness to talk about such a difficult issue." Or, "I appreciate your courage to share your story with me."

> **To validate others is to acknowledge their problems, issues, and feelings—to listen openly and with empathy.**

Sometimes when someone is telling you a story, particularly a personal story, or discusses their frustration, they're looking for you to listen with empathy. Use words of appreciation to demonstrate interest: "That took a lot of courage to tell." "That is really interesting." "Thank you for sharing that with me." When you say these things, showing genuine interest through your tone, they aren't patronizing. People can tell through your body language, tone of voice, and eye contact that you are indeed validating their experience.

Ask probing questions. Every active listener should have an ongoing list of powerful probing questions. Probing questions generate change, connection, introspection, and problem-solving. For example:
- What do you think would happen if . . . ?
- What do you think was the first sign that . . . ?
- What did you learn?
- What would you do differently next time?
- How did you feel when . . . ?
- When she did that, what did you think?

Therapists are experts at asking questions that lead the speaker to come up with their own solutions—self-discovery, their own healing. Clients are really advising themselves.

The questions, of course, can sometimes lead in a certain direction. Questions can be open-ended, closed-ended, or leading. Examples of open-end questions are: "How did you feel?" Or, "What would you do differently next time?" Who, what, when, and where questions allow someone to develop their own response. They don't call for a yes or no. They allow the person to give their own narrative and explanation.

An example of a closed-ended question: "Would you do it that way again, yes or no?" Sometimes, as in this case, it actually asks for a yes or no answer. It's important to create true yes or no questions for people who tend to overexplain. The yes or no answer can take a long conversation and bring it to a point of focus.

Leading questions are, for example, "Did you feel *guilty* setting a boundary for yourself and telling your daughter no?" That question is leading that individual in a particular direction. Other examples: "Did you feel *frustrated* when the manager asked you to clean the restrooms?" "Did you feel *angry* with your coworker for leaving early?" Notice the words "guilty," "frustrated," and "angry" here. You are inserting certain words to lead the conversation to a particular point.

The sixth major step for active listening is the power of silence. Silence can slow down the exchange and reduces discomfort in difficult conversations, providing a space for pauses. The natural space created in the pause gives people an opportunity to diffuse their emotions.

Silence also demonstrates interest. When communicating, people often think they always have to be speaking. They think of communication as a kind of rapid-fire tennis match, with a constant serve and exchange of volleys back and forth until one player has slammed the ball over the net and scored the point. Silence, by contrast, gives an important pause to build connection and allow content to sink in. Don't be afraid to use silence in your communication.

> Don't be afraid to use silence in your communication.

Delivering Effective Feedback

Dr. Susan Baile, author of *Building Self-Esteem in Your Child,* says that giving frequent and meaningful feedback is one of the most powerful tools you have for building self-esteem. When self-esteem is up, performance is up, productivity is up. No matter what our personality style may be, we're all looking for two major things: validation and connection. Active listening is one of the most effective ways to create these feelings.

You often have to give feedback to others. With interactive listening, you begin to do just that. Go beyond mere listening and paraphrasing. Ask questions to go deeper into this process, where you may have to actually provide feedback to someone else.

The feedback process is circular; it's ongoing. You will have to listen, interpret what an individual is saying, and use active listening techniques. Build rapport using the Platinum Rule by trying to treat people the way they want to be treated. Demonstrate emotional intelligence by connecting with the feelings of others. Intuition is one of the greatest assets that you will bring to this process.

Feedback also involves setting smart goals: goals that are specific, measurable, aligned, attainable, realistic, and time-driven. This process builds self-esteem and delivers lasting change. You will use listening as the cornerstone for giving feedback.

Active listening occurs when the listener has little opportunity to respond directly to the speaker. Interactive listening occurs when you can verbally interact with the speaker by asking questions or summarizing. Interactive listening is the process you will use most often.

There are three major techniques that are part of interactive listening: *clarifying, verifying,* and *reflecting*. You've already learned how to reflect by employing mirroring and paraphrasing.

> **Three Major Techniques of Active Listening**
> 1. Clarifying
> 2. Verifying
> 3. Reflecting

Clarifying is another technique you can use. Here you ask questions that fill in details or provide additional information, enabling you to look at all sides of an issue. One simple clarifying question is, "Did I get that right?" You repeat back to the person what you heard using paraphrasing, and then you ask a clarifying question. "Is there more information you will need from me? What specifically did you mean when you said . . . ?" This type of question doesn't challenge or judge the other person or make them defend themselves. It indicates that you are trying to go deeper to understand specifically what they meant. This may enable the person to be more precise and examine their own words more closely.

Verifying is another technique. You repeat back what the other person has said and ask, "Here's what I understood when you said; is that correct?" This enables you to add your understanding of what someone says.

With clarification, you ask the other person to get specific. Verifying is making sure that you have understood: "Here's what I heard when you said you didn't want me to continue to check up on your work. Did you mean that you felt micromanaged by that technique? That's what I heard. Is that correct?"

Sometimes you will use all three of these techniques, initially listening, then paraphrasing back and adding meaning. Go on to ask the person this very powerful question: "Is there more?" They continue to speak.

When they have finished, ask a clarifying question: "What specifically do you need from me in order to feel less frightened?" "When you said that you felt manipulated, what specific actions led you to feel that way?"

Then verifying: "Here's what I heard you say about this. Am I understanding you correctly?"

Feedback builds self-esteem, which is the foundation of human behavior. When you are willing to listen beyond the words to create connection, you are validating the other person's experience and validating them on a personal level.

When you seek to build self-esteem through feedback, you yourself have to demonstrate great courage. In Brené Brown's book *Daring Greatly*, she studies the role of shame in how we communicate with ourselves and how it affects achievement and relationships. She says that the highest demonstration of courage is the willingness to be vulnerable.

The highest demonstration of courage is the willingness to be vulnerable.

If you are going to utilize active listening, you first have to be willing to be vulnerable. Are you willing to walk your own talk? Are you willing to put the problem in front of you and the other person instead of having it *between* you?

You must ask yourself these questions as part of your self-assessment in order to give feedback that doesn't create shame. Most feedback is about shaming or blaming: "Why'd you do it that way?" "What were you thinking?" "What's wrong with you?" For this reason, people shut down: they avoid feedback, they never improve, and they engage in negative and self-destructive behaviors due to shame and blame.

Can you demonstrate the openness you want in return? Use "I" statements instead of "you" statements: "I can see how you might feel . . ." instead of "Why do you feel that way?" Use LB's and NT's: "What did you like best about your performance?" "What was the best part of your day today?" "What would you do differently next time?" You can use these skills in any part of your life.

Going past Shame

Brené Brown created her shame resilience theory in 2006. On her website (positivepsychology.com), she writes, "Shame is the intensely painful feeling or experience of believing that we are flawed and therefore unworthy of love, belonging, and connection," adding that "the fear of shame and judgment is a barrier to communication."

Brown goes on to say that "talking about shame brings a sense of control. That control gives us the strength to overcome our feelings and move forward with our lives."

The experiences that lead many people to feel shame, judgment, and isolation are actually shared, universal experiences. "We all experience shame. It is universal," Brown observes.

Brown says that when we reach out for support, we may receive empathy, which is incompatible with shame and judgment. In fact, empathy is the antidote to the shame and judgment that most people have experienced. You can demonstrate empathy through the listening techniques that you have learned.

If you can learn to listen with empathy, you can create connections. Listening has transformative power. When we listen actively and reflect back to others, showing that we have understood their words and the meaning behind them, we normalize their experience. Instead of launching into autobiographical listening and making it all about us, we are listening to them and saying, "I understand. I validate your experience and where you are."

Nonetheless, sympathy and empathy are completely different. In fact, sympathy can get in the way of demonstrating empathy. Sympathy means feeling the same as someone else: you've had the same experience, the same feeling. You are able to feel what they are feeling. Empathy acknowledges that you cannot feel exactly what someone else is feeling, but you are seeking to connect and understand how they might feel. You are using active listening techniques like paraphrasing, asking thoughtful questions, verifying, and clarifying in order to build connection.

> Empathy acknowledges that you cannot feel exactly what someone else is feeling, but you are seeking to connect and understand how they might feel.

There are times when sympathy might be appropriate. For example, a close friend of yours loses her mother. You have recently gone through the same experience. You share your experience, sympathize, and say, "I'm so sorry. I know how much it hurts to lose your mother." In this case, you truly have had the same experience, and you have something to give. Therefore you might be able to share how you've made it through the stages of grief, helping your friend understand what she might expect.

But sometimes people want empathy rather than sympathy. Even if you've had the same experience, is sharing it going to cause disconnection instead of connection? When you start to share your story, most people have the impression that it's all about you; you are not hearing them.

Whenever possible, try to use empathy instead of sympathy. If you are going to use sympathy, it truly means you feel the same way they feel: "I'm so sorry. I know you are understandably heartbroken. I know exactly how you feel." If you make that statement, have you really had this same experience—and feeling? Will sharing your feelings cause disconnection or connection? What you do have to give could be gained through empathy. Active listening, as we've seen, is an attempt to reflect an understanding, validating the other's experience by paraphrasing, verifying, clarifying, and asking questions instead of getting into the same feeling.

Sympathy can work in support groups, which are targeted for people with very specific similar experiences, so participants can relate and create connection. They have something to give to one another because they've all had to move through and cope with much the same experience.

Not every situation is a support group. When someone is looking for empathy, it can actually cause them to get angry, disconnect, and turn off if you begin to show the same emotion. In any situation, ask yourself whether it calls for sympathy or empathy.

The most powerful tool you have for creating connection is communication, much of will involve giving feedback. Dr. Susan Bale shares some important techniques for giving feedback that creates connection, builds self-esteem, and eliminates shame. We all have an inner critic, our own "not-enough voice," which can get in the way of listening and giving feedback that is effective and validating.

First, check your inner critic, your own not-enough voice. Praise the efforts of others, and not only outcomes. Avoid giving feedback to your children in a way that creates shame. "Why'd you do it like that?" "Why'd you get a C?" "Why'd you get a zero? You are smarter than that. You need to work harder."

Instead, learn to praise efforts. One woman has a son who is a type A thinker, a get it right person, who strives for absolute perfection. His mother wanted to teach him how to manage his inner critic and learn how to praise other achievements, including his efforts. At one point he came to her with a stack of papers and said, "Look, Mom, I got all A's." She replied, "You should feel proud of yourself, and I'm so proud of you, but you know what? I'm not just proud of the A's. I'm really proud of you because you were sick all last week with the flu, but you studied on your own, and you still put in the time to get ready for the test. You got an A even when you were sick." This kind of praise develops a work ethic that children will take with them throughout their lives. Express faith in the other person: "I know that you can do it." "I have confidence in your ability to . . ."

Learn to approve efforts rather than results.

Learn to praise different types of efforts. Speak to what you want rather than what you don't want. Most feedback is about what we *don't* want: "I don't want you to speak to me that way." "I don't want you to keep coming in late. Instead, I want you to arrive on time and be ready to begin work at 9:00 a.m." "I want you to look at me and lower the volume of your voice."

Focus criticism on the behavior, not the person. A lot of feedback is personal. Words like *disrespectful* and *lazy* are interpretations of behaviors. When you give feedback, address the behavior; do not attach your interpretation of that behavior, because that makes it personal.

Also resist the urge to correct grammar. Expertise with grammar and writing is important, but when you correct the grammar of others, they shut down; they feel judged and analyzed, and it does not create connection.

Always remember to use words of courtesy, which opens the lines of communication. Many people want to hear "please" and "thank you"—especially the people people. Some just want you to remember to use their name. Review the techniques we've already discussed for remembering names and faces in order to create connections.

Summary

This chapter described active listening skills to improve communication and remove barriers to listening; the six steps for active listening; how to deliver effective feedback using interactive listening; creating connection; and the difference between sympathy and empathy. The chapter also discussed how to avoid alienating words (such as the accusatory *you*) in verbal communication.

FOUR

Managing Emotions in the Workplace

In a world where things keep getting more challenging, we have tighter time constraints and more trying relationships. Managing everything on your to-do list can create tension. It's all too easy for workplace situations to become emotionally charged. One cross word, bad mood, or mishandled situation can deeply damage a relationship.

In this chapter, we will look at some ways of handling emotions. We're going to start by discussing what emotions are. Then we will move on to anger and what it really means. We'll go on to look at managing emotional balance and staying in control. Next, we'll discuss how to change the way we think. Finally, we'll show to handle emotionally charged situations.

Understanding Emotions

Emotions affect all of us: they make us human. Imagine a world where people didn't experience emotions. It certainly wouldn't be gratifying: no highs, no lows, no disappointment, no excitement. It would almost be like going into a bizarre twilight zone world.

But in the workplace, emotions, especially anger, can cause problems. Often we may feel helpless in the power of emotions, especially when work is piling up, deadlines are getting tight, the sales department is breathing down our neck, and our workload has become overwhelming. But we're not helpless. There's a lot we can do.

Dictionary.com tells us that emotion is a mental state that arises spontaneously rather than through conscious effort. It is often accompanied by changes in physiological feeling. In short, emotions are feelings: in many respects, the words are synonymous.

> Emotion is a mental state that arises spontaneously rather than through conscious effort.

Emotions arise spontaneously, so we can't turn them on or off just because they're producing an effect that we don't want. Producing emotions is not a conscious effort; it is rather like breathing. If you were to stop breathing by consciously deciding, "I'm not going to breathe," what would happen? In a few minutes, you'd pass out, your body would take over, and you'd start to breathe.

Controlling emotions is much the same. When you try to contain them, they build up pressure and eventually erupt. Trying to stop your emotions isn't really managing them: it's merely delaying or ignoring them, so you are only postponing the inevitable.

If ignoring the emotions isn't the solution, we need to look at other ways of handling them. To do so, we need to understand their roots, which is the first key to unlocking the secret of managing them.

Emotional reactions arise from the interactions of three factors: thoughts, feelings, and behavior. Our thoughts affect the way we feel, and our feelings in turn determine how we act, internally or externally. When we look at them in this light, there aren't any bad emotions: they are only appropriate and inappropriate responses.

Unlike emotions, thoughts are conscious: we can control them. To effectively manage our emotions, we must first start by controlling our thoughts.

Let's begin by considering the imaginary case of Bob. Bob works for a medical supply company, and Linda is one of Bob's customers; she works for a skilled nursing facility. Early one morning Bob gets a call from Linda, who is irate. The supplies she ordered have not yet arrived; they're a day late already, and she needs them now.

> To manage your emotions, start by controlling your thoughts.

Bob is mad because he knows he sent the request to shipping. In the back of his mind, he's thinking, "Darn it, they messed up again. Can't they do anything right? When I get hold of them, heads are going to roll." He mutters some excuse to Linda and tries to get to the bottom of the situation. Bob is angry, and Linda has every right to be angry. This is not a progressive or solution-based situation.

Instead of thinking how incompetent the shipping vendor is, let's imagine another way for Bob to solve this problem.

Bob is angry because he did send the request to shipping, but Linda did not get the supplies. At this point he thinks, "I'm not sure what happened, but Linda needs to get the shipment immediately." So he tells her, "Linda, I don't know why you didn't receive the shipment. I'm going to have it shipped overnight as a duplicate order, but we won't charge you for the extra shipping." Bob calls the shipping department to resolve the matter.

In this case, Bob does not direct his anger towards Linda or even toward the shipping department: he finds a solution. By changing his thoughts, Bob produces a more positive outcome.

By simply taking control of our thoughts, we've got more choices. That's one of the first keys to managing our emotions.

Anger and What It Means

Anger is the most destructive emotion. Although it's an ineffective strategy for finding solutions, it rears its ugly head from time to time. Anger can be displayed in the form of outbursts, temper tantrums, name calling, and gossip.

We've already discussed the truth that thought provides the fuel of emotions; therefore it also provides the fuel of anger. What we think increases or decreases the amount of anger we feel (although most of the time, what we're thinking is increasing it).

The second truth is, anger doesn't just happen. People don't go from zero to mad enough to spit bullets in two or three seconds. It builds up over time.

The third truth is that anger is contagious. It's like a disease: it will infect you if you let it. When it happens, you've got trouble.

Three Truths about Anger
1. Thought provides the fuel of anger.
2. Anger doesn't just happen.
3. Anger is contagious

Let's go over some specific tools for overcoming the contagion of anger and avoid infection by other people. Like with anything else, you're going to need to touch up on these techniques from time to time to make sure they're truly working for you.

Anger has a basic equation:

Self-doubt + blame = anger

This equation explains the core of anger in a nutshell. Self-doubt and blame are the two types of thoughts that trigger anger and resentment.

In order to inoculate yourself against explosive emotions, you need to start understanding your own hot buttons. A hot button is a situation or an environment that irritates you: getting stuck in traffic, getting lost, noise, crowds. You can probably find others in yourself without too much difficulty.

Self-doubt + blame = anger

The first key to preventing someone from pushing your hot button is not letting them know where it is. They can't get your goat if they don't know where it's tied up. Protect your hot buttons by identifying where they are beforehand.

One woman has observed that a hot button for her is going to the bank. When she goes to the bank, she's prepared. She has endorsed her checks and has her deposit slips filled out. Inevitably she finds that the person in front of her has no clue about what they're doing: they haven't brought their deposit slips, they can't find their card, they don't have anything together. The woman inevitably finds this frustrating, and it makes her angry.

But the woman stops and thinks about what she's getting mad about. She's getting mad about her own self-doubt: "Why did they do this to me?" She's frustrated and blames the person in front of her: "*They* did it; they set me off."

A similar case is a woman who goes to the grocery store and stands in the express line where customers are supposed to have fourteen items or fewer. But the person in front of her has more than fourteen items. Looking into her thoughts and feelings, she finds that it's really about self-doubt and blame. She thinks, "Why don't *I* use the express lane when my cart is full? Why do I have to follow the rules if they won't?" She goes into the blame game: "It's all the cashier's fault; they let people get away with this stuff."

Another hot button is our expectations of ourselves and others: what we should be able to do, what should happen, or what other people should do. We end up "shoulding" all over the place. We have these feelings because we think things aren't fair: we know how they should be, and we expect them to be that way.

Another trigger is insecurity: the feeling that we didn't measure up, we made a mistake, and we aren't good enough. It could be tied to shame or embarrassment.

The next one is envy and paranoia: the feelings that we are not getting what we deserve and other people are getting something better than we are.

The most common hot button, which usually sets people off faster than any of the others, is not wanting to be responsible and so blaming others. We want a problem to be someone else's fault.

These are some of the most common hot buttons. Take a moment and reflect. Are any of these your hot buttons? Do any of these set you off? Do any of these put you on the path to being angry or upset? If so, jot them down. What are they?

Myths about Anger

Just as there are truths about anger, there are also some myths, and they can be as detrimental to managing your emotions as ignoring the truths.

The first one is, "I can't help it. X makes me so mad." When we blame our anger on someone else, we give them control. You can ask yourself, "How much longer am I going to let them control my life? How much longer am I going to give them that much power?" You may find that you've been giving a lot of other people power in your life, and it's time that you took it back. Understanding this myth gives you permission to take back the reins of your life.

The next myth is somewhat subtler: the person who explodes is angrier than the person who withdraws. This is simply not true. These are two different ways to handle anger. The person who withdraws could actually be much more upset; they're just not showing it.

Myth number three is that anger gets you what you want. In the short term, this might be true, but have you ever been upset with someone or angry with someone, and it ruined the relationship? Did your anger really get you what you wanted? Was it really effective? Anger is a short-term solution for a long-term problem. It may get you what you want in the short term, but it creates a longer-term problem for you. If you don't address the long-term problem, you end up being worse off than if you had addressed it initially.

The fourth myth is that your level of anger reflects how much you are right. Some think that the more you believe in what you're saying, the more you're willing to fight for it. But have you ever met someone who was absolutely dead wrong but was willing to fight to the death about it? It doesn't matter how right or wrong you are: getting angry doesn't solve the issue.

The fifth myth is, "They won't pay attention if I don't make a big deal out of it." This might be true, but think of the boy who cried wolf. He made a big deal out of a false alarm. At first the villagers paid attention to him, but eventually they stopped believing him, even when there actually was a

> **Myths about Anger**
>
> 1. "I can't help it."
> 2. The person who explodes is angrier than the person who withdraws.
> 3. Anger gets you what you want.
> 4. Your level of anger reflects how much you are right.
> 5. They won't pay attention if you don't make a big deal out of it.
> 6. "It's their fault; they should know better."
> 7. "If I suppress my anger and control it, I'll have the upper hand."
> 8. Venting makes you feel better; letting it out is good.

wolf. Did he really get what he wanted? Did he get respect and attention in the long term? Again, short-term actions aren't producing great long-term results.

Myth number six: "It's their fault; they should know better." This issue comes back to being controlled by others and not taking responsibility for our own actions. Yes, others have responsibility for their actions, but we have responsibility for ours as well. When we take back that control, we stop giving other people the right to manipulate us, control us, and push us over the edge. It's our choice, not theirs.

Another myth is, "If I suppress my anger and control it, I'll have the upper hand. I can control it. I'm going to push it down." But you end up becoming resentful and you end up making yourself sick. In her book *Anatomy of the*

Spirit, Caroline Myss, a medical intuitive, says that she can perceive the thoughts that have created specific ailments in the body. This is an interesting area of medicine: maybe it's valid and maybe it isn't. But what if it is true? What if your thoughts really can produce sickness? We need to manage our thoughts; we need to find ways to manage our anger instead of controlling it.

> What if your thoughts really can produce sickness?

Perhaps the biggest myth of them all is, "Venting makes me feel better; letting it out is good." That is a huge whopper. Venting is anger practice, and it forms a habit. We all know how hard habits are to break, so why start with them to begin with?

At this point, we've looked at anger as well as some truths and myths about it. Anger is actually natural. It's part of who we are. Therefore it is not a great solution to suppress or ignore anger. Instead, we need to learn how to manage it.

When Is Anger a Problem?

Before we decide to manage anger, let's decide whether it is a problem or not. Anger is a problem when it's frequent. Is there anger or hostility at your workplace every day? Is it intense? If someone's level of anger doesn't quite seem to match the cause, there may be an issue that needs to be looked at.

Anger's a problem when it lasts a long time. Say you forgot to bring your agenda to a meeting a month ago and your supervisor's still holding that over your head. Anger is a problem when it's aggressive, cruel, destructive, or hostile. Are you afraid, either physically or mentally, to go to work? Do team members talk down or bad-mouth each other?

Anger could be a problem when it places control over solutions—for example, when decisions are made with a sense of "I won, you lost," or some ridiculous policy is in effect in your office because someone threw a tantrum.

Finally, anger is a problem when it interferes. Are you stressed every day? Are you forgetful? Are you having difficulty doing your job? If you've answered yes to any of these, anger could be a problem in your workplace.

The tips here are not designed to handle an entire environment full of anger. Your team or company may need additional training or an entire shift in culture. Many companies have early intervention programs (EIPs) that offer help for these situations. If you are experiencing many or most of these characteristics at work, reach out to your human resources (HR) professional and see what help is available.

Anger and Communication

We communicate in three different ways. Let's briefly look at these ways and how we can see anger through each of them.

The first type of communication is verbal: the words we say. Someone who is angry might say something like, "Nobody treats me like that," "I'm not taking this lying down," or,

"Who do you think you are?" These would indicate that this person is angry.

The second type of communication is paraverbal. Here it's not the words we say: it's how we say them. Take this sentence, said with emphasis on each of the three words: "*I'm* not angry." "I'm *not* angry. "I'm not *angry*." Each of these conveys different emotional responses, although the words are identical.

Here's a common example. You pass a colleague in the hallway and ask, "How are you?" Your colleague responds, "I'm fine." Simple, right? But they could be saying that in a way that you believe or in a way that you don't believe. That's paraverbal communication.

What's important to remember about paraverbal communication is that when you say something, the receiver of that message is more likely to trust your paraverbal messages over your actual words. This means that how you say something is even more important than what you say.

The third form of communication is one we've already discussed: body language, which communicates feelings, emotions, attitudes, and thoughts. Your body movements are all part of your body language, including your gestures, postures, facial expressions, smiling, frowning, crossing your arms, rolling your eyes, standing with your hands behind your back, pointing at someone when you talk, and biting your lip. Some of these, such as standing with your arms behind your back, are inviting gestures, while others, such as folding your arms across your chest, can be closed or defensive gestures. Various forms of body language can indicate anger and should be noted by the recipient.

> **Three Forms of Communication**
> 1. Verbal
> 2. Paraverbal
> 3. Body language

Paraverbal communication doesn't exist in written messages, and body language doesn't exist in written messages or audio communication. If you are on a teleconference with audio only, you can't see the way others are sitting or the way they look; you can't read any of that body language. All you have to go by to determine their emotional state are the words they're saying and the tone of their voice. If you work on virtual teams, you want to keep this fact in mind.

In certain teleconference meetings, the participants in the company's main location on the East Coast seemed bothered that they had to teleconference with team members on the West Coast. The Easterners were inflecting their voices in such a way that was causing irritation to the people on the West Coast. After a lot of debate, aggression, and heated discussions, the management team took a look at the situation. They discovered that because of the time difference, the employees on the East Coast had to stay later than their usual hours, so they were run down, frustrated, and worn out, whereas those on the West Coast were only halfway through their day. They were still peppy and full of energy. Paraverbal communication was interfering with verbal communication. Management realized that if they could move the time up earlier in the day, everybody would be in a better mood, and the calls became much more productive.

Knowing these types of communication and being able to read them can help you identify a potentially explosive situation well before it detonates. When you are the one sending the message, being aware of your verbal and paraverbal communication and body language enables you to communicate the proper message and emotions.

Maintaining Emotional Balance

As we've seen, ignoring emotions does not lead to effective results, so we must learn to manage our emotions. This process starts with recognizing the warning signs. Remember, anger doesn't just happen. Sometimes you can recognize symptoms that anger is building up in yourself. They include shortness of breath, tight chest, throbbing temples, rising heart rate, increased blood pressure, knotted stomach, adrenaline rush, a weakness in the knees, sweating, a clenched jaw, and a pounding chest.

When you recognize these symptoms, you can take control and start to manage them. You can stop an emotionally charged situation before it ever starts. But in order to do that, you need to control the physical symptoms. There are many options: You can get out of the situation; you can do conscious breathing or conscious relaxation. You can unclench your jaw, stretch, and lower your voice. You can do all of these things to take back control of yourself.

Let's try a quick relaxation exercise that you can use to alleviate symptoms of anger. You can do it in a number of

> **Warning Signs of Anger**
> - Shortness of breath
> - Tight chest
> - Throbbing temples
> - Rising heart rate
> - Increased blood pressure
> - Knotted stomach
> - Adrenaline rush
> - Weakness in the knees
> - Sweating
> - Clenched jaw
> - Pounding chest

ways: you can read the book and follow the directions step by step; you can read it aloud, record it, and play it back as you do the exercise; or you can have a partner and read it to each other in turn.

Begin by tensing up: raise your shoulders up to your ears; tense your body. Hold it for several seconds, then let go.

Now close your eyes and slowly take a breath in as you count to 10. Breathe so deeply that both your chest and your abdomen move in and out. Take a breath in: 1, 2, 3, 4, 5, 6, 7, 8, 9, 10. Now very slowly breathe out: 1, 2, 3, 4, 5, 6, 7—feel yourself relaxing—8, 9, 10.

This time as you breathe in, relax your eye muscles: 1, 2, 3. Feel your eye muscles relaxing: 4, 5. Slowly unclench your jaw: 6, 7. Feel all the muscles in your face starting to relax: 8. Breathe in: 9, 10. Go ahead and exhale.

Now go ahead and breathe in again: 1, start to relax your shoulders; 2, feel the tension going away; 3, your arms are getting heavy: 4, 5, 6. Let your hands relax: 7, 8. Now relax your chest and abdomen, breathe in, breathe out, breathe in, breathe out.

Open your eyes. How do you feel? Are you a little bit more relaxed, a little less tense, a little less edgy? Controlling your breath is one key way to change your mood and release negativity.

Another, somewhat longer practice: With each breath, slowly work on relaxing your muscles. Start from your head and work all the way down to your toes. Generally, the recommended time frame for this type of relaxation exercise is about ten minutes. If you are not patient enough for that at the start, you might want to start at two minutes. Then each week add a minute and slowly work your way up to ten minutes.

Use regular relaxation exercises to manage anger.

Ideally, you should book ten minutes of this practice into your day. It will help you to become more relaxed and more in control. If you have an hour for lunch, take fifteen minutes for the relaxation practice. If you schedule a half hour to review the agenda for weekly meetings, schedule twenty minutes instead. This practice is important not only to your relationships and your career, but to your health.

One recent study indicates that despite gains in medicine and nutrition, the average American working in a corporate environment is not as healthy as his or her counterpart from thirty years ago. Much of this decline has been attributed to mental health. So even if you can't get a full ten minutes for your relaxation practice, do as much as you can, because the benefits will be worth it. If you choose not to schedule this time, at least keep your mind free so you can do something to reduce and let go of fear and concern.

Once you get good at this practice, you may grow bored with it. There are many variations. For example, some people, when they breathe in and breathe out, say, "Relax" silently or aloud in a whisper when they exhale.

If you need more suggestions, try this website: meditationcenter.com. It's a free website, and you can go there to get several relaxation techniques. Many of them will work extremely well in an office setting.

Conscious relaxation works on many levels. It works physiologically—it slows down your heart, relaxes your muscles, and helps you feel better—but it works psychologically as well. It slows down your thoughts and reactions, reduces anxiety, and puts you in a position to break free of your anger and take back control of yourself.

Changing the Way You Think

A key to controlling your emotions is changing the way you think. Remember, thoughts create feelings, which create behaviors. In order to change a feeling, we have to first change the thought.

Despite the complexities of our brains, it's nearly impossible to think about two things at once, especially when you focus on one of two thoughts. Conscious breathing makes you focus on the breathing, on relaxing your muscles. It draws attention away from the hot buttons that someone has just pushed. Moreover, because our thoughts affect the way we feel, changing thoughts automatically changes the way we feel.

There are several ways to change your thoughts. The first one, which we've just been talking about, is to think of something else. You don't need to do anything fancy here. Whenever your hot button is pushed, think of something different: where you're going to spend your vacation; what you want for lunch today; or how your favorite sports team did last night. It really doesn't matter what you think about; you just need to think about something different than the hot button. Hot buttons are fuel for angry thoughts.

> One way to manage anger is simply to think of something else.

There may be times when you can't conjure up any relaxing images. In that case, you can fall back onto the second concept: simply to use the word *stop*. Every time you find yourself with a thought that's blocking you from coping or controlling your anger, just say, "Stop." If you're by yourself, you can say it out loud. If you are around other people, you say can it silently. If the thought comes back, say, "Stop" again. Eventually the disturbing thought will go away.

Other methods: You can try to divert your attention with something that requires concentration, such as work. You can also listen to music that relaxes you.

Trying to change your thoughts may seem to be much easier said than done. But as you practice some of these techniques over time, they become habits, and new habits create new thoughts, new emotions, and new behaviors.

The next time you get a particularly annoying email, instead of getting frustrated or mad, try consciously relaxing: stop and listen to some music. Divert your attention. Don't focus on the email; focus on something else.

But what do you do if someone is right there in front of you? What do you do if they're in your face? Say you're having a conversation with someone, and it starts to get heated; that person says the most ridiculous thing you've ever heard. You can't just walk away and go listen to some music. In those cases, you need something special and fast acting and something you can do without adding fuel to the fire.

In this case, simply count to ten. No doubt you've heard this before (your childhood teacher was right). If you're listening to someone and getting upset, pause mentally in the back of your mind and distract yourself by counting to ten. Don't do it out loud. The other person shouldn't see your lips moving.

When all else fails, say something like, "You know what? I'm going to need a little bit of time." Take a walk, get a drink of water; count to ten while you're away; calm yourself down.

When all else fails, say, "I'm going to need a little time" and leave the situation.

Have you ever been in a situation where you didn't take that time, the situation escalated, and you said some things that you didn't mean? You may have even burned a bridge that you didn't want to burn. It's very easy to do that. When we get into heated arguments, we can be pushed over the edge. Before we know it, we're saying things that we really don't want to be saying, and we're burning bridges that may take us days, weeks, months, or years to repair. We may never be able to repair some of those bridges. So take the time to count to ten.

These are two techniques for calming down in the heat of the battle. The first is a timeout: walk away; remove yourself. The second is counting to ten.

Another important point: people used to be told to get it out of their system, to let it all out. Sometimes they were encouraged to express their anger aggressively. But think about this approach. Does it make sense? Would you tell a smoker who's trying to quit but is having a craving for a cigarette to get it out of their system and have a cigarette? That's merely reinforcing that behavior.

The science backs it up as well. Studies now indicate that practiced aggression does not dissipate anger. Aggressive behavior reinforces aggression. In other words, if we act aggressively, we become more aggressive.

Up to this point, we've talked about how to keep from losing your cool, but even with all of the techniques we've discussed, we're still human. It may happen. There may be times when one of our hot buttons is pushed and we fly off the handle. It can and most likely will happen. But if you ever do explode, don't be passive and just let the pieces fall where they may. The damage could certainly be permanent. You want to be active and earn back some credibility in those broken relationships.

Handling Emotionally Charged Situations

Let's go back to Bob. He's fuming because the shipment was not sent to his client. He calls the shipping manager to complain, and the manager assures him that all the orders are double-checked and that Bob must have made a mistake.

Bob certainly doesn't want to hear that. He raises his voice and lets the manager know that he shouldn't tell him how to do his job. "It's not my fault you hired incompetent employees. Get it fixed, or I'll talk to your boss myself." He slams the phone down without even waiting for a response.

How did Bob handle that situation on a scale of 1 to 10, 1 being horrible, 10 being excellent? It was probably closer to the 1 than to the 10. Did he handle it as well as he could have? He flew off the handle and certainly did not build any relationships with that manager.

With a few extra skills, Bob might be able to handle that conversation a little better next time.

The first step is to admit your mistake. Acknowledge that the action was not productive.

The second step is to address the problem. This means asking questions in order to obtain information that will help solve the real issue, not the emotional issue.

Third, disassociate from criticism. Use a SMART action plan to solve the problem.

SMART is an acronym. Your action plan should be *specific, measurable, achievable, rewarding,* and *time-specific*. It's also monitored with those that are involved.

Step number four is to ask yourself what you learned from this situation.

Step five: let go and forgive yourself.

The SMART Action Plan
- Specific
- Measurable
- Achievable
- Rewarding
- Time-specific

Let's see what happens when we teach Bob these five steps. After Bob has his little outburst, he goes off and thinks about things. He realizes that his tantrum didn't solve the issue. If anything, it damaged his relationship with the shipping manager. Bob goes for a walk, calms down, and decides to resolve the situation. He comes up with a plan and calls the shipping manager back. Now of course the shipping manager isn't excited to hear back from Bob so quickly, but Bob starts with step one. He apologizes for his outburst, then he moves to step number two. He explains that the orders to his clients have not been going out on time or correctly. The manager acknowledges that this is true.

Bob asks why the manager thought this was happening. The manager doesn't have any explanation, so he and Bob pull a copy of Bob's order form. The general information that Bob provided was on the first page, but when Bob referred to page two, the manager said there was no page two. Through discussion, they determined that the online order form was being cut off after the first page. Their orders were being cut short.

Step number three: Bob ignores the manager's criticism that Bob's department created the form, so he's to be blamed for failing to catch the error. Instead they work out a SMART action plan addressing how and when the form will be reformatted so that the entire form will go through to shipping.

Bob calls his customer back and explains the situation. She isn't entirely happy that it happened, but she is glad that she will be getting her order correctly going forward. She is also happy that he has made up for the omission by making the order overnight without charging her.

Step number four: Bob realizes that mistakes happen, and for about two weeks after the change, he copies himself on all the orders just to make sure the order form isn't being cut off.

On step number five, the shipping manager is short with Bob for a while, but Bob lets the issue go. Soon the manager does too, and the business relationship resumes as normal.

The Faces of Anger

We can see that by following the step-by-step guide, we can do our best to salvage an outburst. But what can you do when it's not your outburst, it's somebody else's? How can we deal with conflict when it's staring us in the face? How do we resolve issues so that anger does not become a recurring problem in our office?

Angry people have many different tactics for drawing us into their world of anger. By understanding these tactics, you can quickly identify them and inoculate yourself to their allure.

The first has to do with the faces of anger: aggressive, passive, and passive-aggressive. We often consider exploding anger as the scariest or the hardest to deal with. However, concealed anger is much more difficult to recognize, because people mask it.

> **Three Faces of Anger**
> - Passive
> - Aggressive
> - Passive-aggressive

All three of these behaviors are win-lose or lose-lose approaches to anger. As we review them, think about each of them and how it's demonstrated. Jot down next to them any time that you may use this style.

We need to become conscious of what we are doing in order to be able to change it. Of course, we also want to recognize what others are doing as well. Keep your eyes and ears open.

The first type is *aggression*. It's the hot face of anger, right there in the open. Some people are addicted to anger. Aggressive people blow up. It's a tool to get what they want. Aggression is blaming, attacking, and criticizing, and people can act aggressive when they feel criticized, put down, or shamed. Aggressive people use anger as a means of power and control. They use it to intimidate. They may have the intent to harm.

Aggressive behavior is based on the feeling that you must be strong and in control and must not compromise. These people may be thinking, "Winning is everything. I have to stay on my guard. People are trying to take things that are mine." Blowing up keeps them from having to deal with the true issues at hand.

Let's go back to Bob. He's in the office, and he's got another problem. A colleague in the next cubicle listens to music too loud. Bob's upset because he's under pressure to get a deadline completed. But he can't focus, because it sounds as if there's a block party going on next door. Bob yells over his cube, "Turn that down. Are you deaf or just dumb? This is a business." The music instantly turns off. What's the outcome of this exchange? Bob got his needs met, but at the expense of his colleague.

Let's look at the next face of anger, which is *passive*. Passive people repress or internalize anger. They withdraw to avoid any conflict. These people often fear loss of control or rejection. They hide any disagreement. As a result, they don't get their needs met (which can actually make them sick). People who fear anger often hide from it. They avoid dealing with issues by withdrawing or acting helpless. Sometimes they project their anger onto others, and they may direct their anger towards themselves as well.

What would happen if Bob reacted passively to his noisy neighbor? He's upset because he has some important deadlines and can't focus because of the block party in the next cubicle. Bob doesn't say anything. He just pouts in his cubicle, trying to figure out what he can do if he can't tune out the noise and focus on his own. Bob decides that he deserves whatever reprimand the supervisor gives him.

What's the outcome of this exchange? Bob doesn't get his needs met. He accommodates his colleague at his own expense. The colleague doesn't even have any idea that Bob is upset.

The third style is the *passive-aggressive*. Passive-aggressive behavior is expressing anger indirectly in ways such as sarcasm. Passive-aggressive people will suddenly be late. They'll "accidentally" lose or forget something. They use paraverbal communication or body language to act angry, but they don't acknowledge their anger.

Passive-aggressive behavior can be sneaky. This type of person can be extremely angry while acting as if they're not angry at all. Although they don't admit that they're angry, they enjoy making others pay. They often say yes when they mean no, but people figure out what's going on because the anger leaks out in other ways.

In this case, if Bob's stressing over his tight deadlines, the next time the music is roaring in his neighbor's cubicle, Bob doesn't say anything. People can tell something's bothering him, but he denies it. He just says, "Oh, I didn't sleep well," but he obsesses over the music all day. The next morning, he brings in a CD called *American Idol: The Worst Auditions Ever* and plays it all morning at a ridiculous decibel level. By lunchtime the entire department is mumbling.

What is the outcome here? Bob still isn't getting his needs met, and he's doing his darndest to make sure nobody else is either.

What are the outcomes for expressing anger in these ways? If you're aggressive, you get your own needs met, but at the expense of others. If you're passive, you accommodate others at your own expense. If you're passive-aggressive, no one gets their needs met.

All these approaches have one thing in common: the inability to perceive things honestly, clearly, and objectively. It doesn't matter how we express it, whether we're hotheaded or withdrawn: our thinking becomes irrational and distorted. Until we can gain control of our thoughts, it's going to be difficult to have any positive outcomes.

Distorted thinking is another tactic used by angry people. It can come in the form of filters, whereby they only focus on things that build their case. Then we have polarity: perceptions that grow farther and farther apart. The problem becomes all-or-nothing. There is personalizing: "That's how people *should* act." There's also exaggerating—magnifying the intensity or degree of the problem. Labeling is another tactic: generalizing, placing everything into a single category. Finally, there is mind reading: when you think you know

---

Tactics of Distorted Thinking

- Filters: focusing only on things that build your case
- Polarity
- Personalizing
- Exaggerating
- Labeling
- Mind reading

exactly what people are thinking, and especially what they are thinking about you.

When people use distorted thinking to build their case, they try to lure you into their thinking. When confronting an angry person, it doesn't matter if the style is passive, aggressive, or passive-aggressive: you don't want to feed into distorted thinking. They're not thinking clearly, and they will try to suck you in too.

You don't want that to happen. You have to maintain control by counting to ten, saying stop, or backing yourself out of the situation. You want to have a clear success plan about what to do when you encounter these situations.

The Assertive Style

At this point, we can look back at these faces of anger. Do you fit into any of these categories? Perhaps it depends on your audience. Maybe you're passive with your boss but aggressive with your coworkers. Maybe you don't fit into one of these models at all, because there's a fourth approach that differs from all of them.

We're all born either passive, aggressive, or passive-aggressive. That's in our nature. But the fourth model is learned. To be effective in handling our emotions, we need to learn this fourth approach, which is called *assertive*. It can be described as expressive, respectful, confident, open, and productive. Assertive people express anger when it's worthwhile to do so. They're able to say what they want and describe a situation objectively without assigning blame.

> **The Assertive Style**
> - Expressive
> - Respectful
> - Confident
> - Open
> - Productive

When they express themselves and communicate, they do so openly and respectfully, and it's productive.

Seeking to get your needs met while respecting the needs of others is the key to being assertive. It's upholding your rights without disrespecting the rights of others. As we approach anger assertively, we work to meet our own needs without stepping on the rights of others.

There's a simple script that you can use to be assertive when dealing with anger: "I feel (insert emotion) because I think (insert what you think), and what I would like is (insert what you want)." It might sound like this: "I feel frustrated when you get up and leave when we're talking, because I think you're not interested in what I'm saying. I would like you to listen and wait until I'm done speaking before you can get up and leave." This is a very simple formula for being assertive when you encounter the anger of other people.

Let's go back to Bob. The next time the neighbor's music comes up, Bob goes over to his colleague and says, "I feel distracted and stressed with my workload when you have your music turned up so loud because I think—well, I *can't* think. I'm not going to be able to meet my deadlines. I would like you to turn the music down so I can't hear it."

Bob's neighbor apologizes. He tells him he had no idea that anyone had a problem with his music. He thought everyone in the department liked the music, which was why he had it turned up so loud. He says he'll keep it down from now on.

It was that simple. Bob just needed to ask for what he wanted. Let's look at the outcome here. Bob's needs are met. He can get his work done, and he respects the needs of the other person, who can still listen to the music, but at a lower volume. It's a win-win situation.

As long as people are people, there's going to be anger, but there are positive ways of handling it. Let's explore some other tips.

1. Focus on the issue, not the person. This isn't a time for name calling or blaming.
2. Focus specifically on the issue. Talk about one issue at a time. Don't talk about the past or things that have happened before.
3. Make sure to hear each other out. Take time to listen in order to get all the information and understand the real concerns.
4. Start by assuming everyone has good intentions.
5. Enforce the right to disagree. It's OK if you don't agree with everything they say.
6. Pit people against problems and not against other people.
7. Explore the problem before generating solutions. This means truly understanding what the real issue is. Once

you do, these rules of thumb will make it much easier to resolve the problem.

8. Focus on the interests, not the position.
9. Focus on the benefits. What are the benefits of resolving this issue?
10. Use "I" statements. Avoid "you" statements: "You said this; you did that." Instead say, "When you said X, I heard . . ." This is much less blaming and allows the other person to communicate much more freely.
11. Avoid your hot buttons. If you know where they are, try to stay out of those situations.
12. Pay attention to your paraverbal communication and body language, which, as you'll remember, are really your main communication tools. If someone is listening to you, they're going to pay more attention to how you said it than what you said.
13. Be careful of your sighs. These are huge red flags of anger and frustration.
14. Keep your hands to yourself. Sometimes putting our hands too close to other people incites anger. You want to keep your hands within your close body sphere.
15. Make sure you're conveying interest, but don't be patronizing. Nobody wants to be patronized. It comes off as sarcastic rather than sincere.

Three Different Approaches

At this point, let's put these rules together to create some approaches that you can use. There are many approaches to dealing with emotions. Of course, not every one is going to work in every situation, and not every one works with every person, so we'll look at three approaches. If you like one, keep it; if you don't, try something else.

The first approach comes from Stephen Covey's *Seven Habits of Highly Effective People*, and we've already encountered it. He calls it "seeking first to understand." This is where we listen, ask questions, and blend. Listening involves tuning into what's happening. Covey suggests we go further and listen empathetically. Don't just listen actively; listen so that you can put yourself in the other person's place with empathy. Eliminate your story. Forget what you would do or how you would think. Just listen and make use of active nonverbal messages. Be aware of your tone and body language. Listen to the other person's tone and body language. What are they really saying? What are their silent motivators? Maybe lean forward a little to let them know you're really paying attention.

The second approach is to ask questions and encourage logical thinking. You could ask, "What evidence is there towards this? Are there any exceptions? Do all the facts support this? What are the chances that will happen?"

The second approach is broken down into five specific steps.

1. Stay calm. You need to stay in control of yourself so that someone else's anger doesn't infect you.
2. Take the other person's emotions seriously. Don't blow them off. Don't act as if they're joking. That's not going to help.
3. Help them cool off. Provide physical and emotional outlets. Allow them to talk. Allow them to speak. Speaking

> **Three Approaches to Dealing with Emotions**
> 1. Seek first to understand.
> 2. Ask questions; encourage logical thinking
> 3. Get in step with the other person.

slower can help them slow down as well. But be careful: don't say, "Calm down." This is one of the worst things you can do to help them cool off. If you need to take a break, do so, but again make sure to go back to deal with the real situation.

4. Be assertive and uphold your rights. You don't want to be defensive or aggressive, but it's not helpful to come across as passive or intimidated.
5. Move to a constructive discussion and problem-solving. Ask how the situation can be solved immediately. What's the best thing to do? But you don't want to move towards solving or suggesting until you've actually listened.

The third approach is to get in step with the other person. You want to find things in common. Use common language: it will help to build rapport and overcome the challenge at hand.

This is the same approach as suggested when dealing with managing your own emotions. The only difference here is we've eliminated step number one, which is apologizing.

When anger flares up at work, you can use these three techniques as a quick reference. Have them available in your top drawer. Review them from time to time. Remember, anger is infectious, but you can inoculate yourself from it if you have the tools and you continue to review them on a regular basis.

Summary

In this chapter, we started with understanding emotions and went to understanding anger and what it means. Then we discussed maintaining emotional balance and staying in control, going on to changing the way we think. Finally, we dealt with handling emotionally charged situations.

FIVE

Confronting Workplace Conflict

Is conflict running rampant in your workplace? If it's allowed to grow unchecked, workplace conflict drags down morale, creates tension and frustration, gets in the way of productivity, and poisons work relationships.

Clearly you want to reduce the amount of conflict occurring in your workplace, but how do go about it? How do you deal with aggressive behavior, negative attitudes, excessive sarcasm, hidden agendas, and other sources of workplace conflict in a positive, healthy, and productive fashion? How can you diffuse the hot-button situations, calm explosive personalities, and exercise damage control without losing your own confidence and composure?

In this chapter, we'll start by understanding conflict. What is it? What causes it? Where's the root of it? We will proceed to talk about adjusting to different personality styles. Then we'll look at effective listening skills and how they drastically affect the outcome of a conflict. Then we will move on to discuss how to conquer and tame toxic types. We'll conclude by going over the six steps to conflict management.

Understanding Conflict

There are multiple causes of conflict. The first is misunderstandings. Sometimes we misinterpret what somebody is saying in a conversation; sometimes misperceptions result from rumors in the office gossip mill. In any event, they can cause conflict, making people feel attacked or blamed.

Causes of Conflict
- Misunderstanding
- Fear
- Confusion
- Difference of opinion

In addition to misperception, there is a second cause, which is fear. Sometimes we're afraid of failure, we're afraid of change, we're not sure what's going to happen, and that scares us. This creates confusion. Confusion can also cause conflict: not knowing what's happening or not understanding why something is happening.

Then of course there's difference of opinion. Sometimes this occurs because we're passionate about what we think, and sometimes it's because we're not open to other possibilities.

All of these situations can lead to conflict. Each of us handles conflict differently, because our thought and communication processes vary considerably.

Stop and consider the possible causes behind the conflict that you might be encountering. Is it misunderstanding? Has someone said something that was not properly understood? Is it fear? Is it confusion, misperception, or maybe difference of opinion? Once we understand the causes, we can consider how to resolve the conflict.

Think about conflicts you've been involved in. Most of the time, is the result positive or negative? You will probably find that most of the time the results are negative. That's why we often avoid talking about conflict, but until we start to discuss and understand it, we can't resolve it or move forward.

Unfortunately, ignoring conflict doesn't make it go away. Usually, conflict ignored gets bigger; it becomes more of an issue. It's like the proverbial 800-pound elephant sitting in the room: everybody knows it's there, but nobody's talking about it.

Our first step to handling conflict, then, is to understand it. We want to start by looking at the root cause. If you're currently involved in a conflict, make a commitment today that you're going to address it, whatever it is. Below we will discuss a step-by-step process to resolve conflict. But sticking your head in the sand certainly won't resolve it.

Adjusting to Personality Styles

At this point you undoubtedly recognize that different people have different styles. There are many systems for categorizing these styles, with different numbers of types—commonly four, although there may be as many as sixteen.

We've already gone over one system of understanding personality styles in chapter 3, but we can review them briefly from a slightly different perspective. There are four:

1. **Thinkers**, as their name suggests, like to think. They like to get it right. They are often engineer types or people that like to work with numbers.

2. **Relaters** are people people. They often have candy on their desks, they're always there to help others, and they love being a part of a team.

Both of these types are passive in that they dislike conflict and withdraw at all costs to avoid it. Relaters avoid conflict by placating. They tend to give in to the other person so they don't have to deal with a conflict. Thinkers, on the other hand, withdraw and go off to think. If they don't want to be confronted, they'll often say, "You know what? I have to think about that." They'd rather think about the issue than suggest something that could cause a conflict.

The following two styles are more aggressive. They are less prone to avoiding conflict, although they approach it in different ways.

3. **Socializers** are upbeat, high-energy people. They tend to be excitable and extraverted. They tend to avoid conflict by promoting their ideas. They'll often talk louder than others; they'll get more and more excited about their ideas, and they'll try to convince others that their way is the right way.

4. **Directors** are more task-oriented—not quite as high-energy as socializers, but certainly very strong personalities. They tend to say, "Get it done." They avoid conflict by always having the answers. They know what needs to get done, they're highly confident, and sometimes their high confidence level strays over into overconfidence. They avoid conflict by becoming more confident than anyone else. Other people tend to give in to them so they don't have to deal with any clashes.

> You will handle conflict differently depending on your personal style.

If you're involved in a conflict right now, stop and think about what style are you dealing with. You will handle it differently depending on the style. A director, being strong, bold, and in your face, may try to convince you that his answer is right. The relater may just say, "OK, you're right." Often what works with the director will not work with the relater, and what works with thinkers won't work with socializers.

Communication Styles

In short, you want to start thinking about the style of the person you are encountering and how you need to address it. So let's take a look at the communication styles as well.

As we've already observed, there are three communication styles: passive, aggressive, and passive-aggressive.

Passive communicators tend to give in even to the point of violating their own rights. They tend to let others have their way and sometimes turn into doormats. In a conflict with a passive communicator, if you act strong and try to convince them, they're likely to lie down and say, "OK, you're right." A strong approach is unlikely to work with them.

Aggressive communicators tend to walk on the rights of others. They make sure their rights are respected, but they may try to take advantage of other people's rights. You can be a little stronger with aggressive people. Certainly you would never want to get into an arguing match, but you can be a bit stronger with this style.

With the passive-aggressive person, nobody's rights are respected. They may lie down when confronted by conflict and appear to agree, even if they don't. The passive-aggressive communication style often comes out when the individual they're dealing with has a stronger personality than they do. A socializer or relater can quickly become passive-aggressive when in conflict with a director. They're unlikely to go head-to-head against this style. They might appear to agree in person but will try to have their way afterward, when the conflict seems to be over.

Obviously none of these three communication styles is satisfactory. In conflict, no matter which style you are dealing with, basic skills start with being assertive. Being assertive means that you respect the other person's rights, assure them that they're being heard, and empower them to envision a win-win situation.

Some assertive skills are very effective in managing conflict. Let's take a look at a couple of them.

Basic communication skills start with an assertive stance.

We've already gone into detail about one of the most important tools in managing conflict: listening. When we're communicating, we tend to want to state our side, our point of view, and express what we're thinking and feeling. This impulse tends to be stronger than wanting to hear the other side. But if you don't allow the other person to be heard, they can feel taken advantage of. Listening to them empowers us to start envisioning a win-win situation. If we know somebody else's wants and needs, we can start thinking about how to balance them with what we want or need, so we can anticipate possible win-win outcomes.

Moreover, once we have heard and understood the other person, they're more likely to hear and understand us.

Let's go into a technique that can be very effective in communication, particularly in conflict situations.

Imagine that someone in the workplace comes up to you and says, "You make me so mad! You messed up. You made a huge mistake. Now we have to spend time and money fixing it."

What is happening in your mind when someone comes at you with that approach? Generally, the first thing we start to feel is shutting our brain down. We stop listening. We're thinking of other things, focusing somewhere else.

What has been said that causes this kind of reaction? When somebody says "you," it feels like an attack. It puts us on the defense. We feel we have to defend who we are and what we're thinking and saying. Or we feel, "No, wait a minute, that wasn't me." In any event, we don't really listen to the rest of what's being said.

> When someone says "you," it feels like an attack.

Also, as we've already seen, if you say to somebody, "You make me mad," can that person really make you mad? If you tell them they made you mad, you've given them control over what you're feeling. How much control do you really want to give to other people?

Assertive communication uses an approach that makes sure that we can keep the door open for the communication process while keeping control of our emotions within ourselves. We can have the wherewithal to say, "I'm mad when the project gets messed up, because now we're going to have to spend money fixing it." Using the words "I," "when," and "because" works extraordinarily well and produces phenomenal results. But what words have you changed? You've principally changed one word: instead of saying "you," you said "I." This allows the other person to hear what you're going to say without putting barriers up and turning their listening off. Now you have an opportunity for conversation.

Using "I" also means that you're stating your feelings: "My emotions are mine, and I'm not going to blame somebody else for them. I'm going to maintain control of myself."

Of course, we can also say, "I'm mad at you." We're back to ground zero, because, again, you've said "you." Don't say the word *you*. Avoid the word *you*. The more you can stay away from it—especially at the beginning of the sentence—the more open the conversation will be, and the easier it will be to resolve conflicts and move forward.

Four Powerful Questions

In a conflict, have you ever noticed that we tend to say, "Whose fault is it? Who said that? Who did it?" We end up trapped in the sea of blame and the game of pointing fingers, and it's ineffective. We're not getting the results we want. Instead, you want to focus on what's happening; where do we need to go?

Here is a series of four different questions that you can apply to start focusing on the results and where you're going instead of pointing fingers at each other.

1. **Where are we right now?** It doesn't matter who said it, who did it, or whose fault it is. What really counts is where things are right now. Once we understand this, we have a chance to move forward.
2. **Where do we need to go?** What are we trying to accomplish? This is our focus.
3. **What actions do we need to take to get there?** We have to get specific. What is it going to take? What do we

> **Four Questions for Disarming Conflict**
> 1. Where are we right now?
> 2. Where do we need to go?
> 3. What actions do we need to take to get there?
> 4. How can we prevent this problem in the future?

need to have to do? Who's going to take what steps to achieve the results we're looking for?

4. **How can we prevent this problem in the future?** Whatever the situation is, we need to anticipate it. If it's going to come up again, we need to make sure it won't be a problem in the future.

By wrapping our conversation around these four questions, we're setting up an opportunity to say, "OK, whatever this conflict is, let's work out where we want to take it, where we want to go, and how we can become more effective in the outcome."

Listening Skills Revisited

We went into some detail about listening skills in chapter 3, but let's quickly review the key points.

First, listening skills are key. Not only do we need assertive communication—which is how we say what we say—we need to make sure we're listening effectively to be able to move through the conversation. So let's look at the key listening skills we're going to need in a conflict situation. The first

> **Skills for Disarming Conflict**
> 1. Active listening
> 2. Rephrasing
> 3. Reflective listening

one is *active listening*. As we've seen, this means having eye contact with the other person—letting them know with our eyes that you're really listening. It's also about body language. For example, if we cross our arms in a conflict, the other person might think we're angry, closed off, and shutting down, and we don't want to hear what they're saying. We're sending a certain signal. In a case like that, we're not going to get very far in our conflict. We need to make sure that we have awareness: What is my body language? What is the message that I'm sending to anybody else? Then we open up. Make sure you're not crossing your arms or legs and you're sitting in a relaxed position. You're not in attack or defense mode, and you're listening to what they have to say.

The next key is *rephrasing*. Rephrasing is restating what the other person is saying to make sure we understand it. Here we want to use a few of their key words—not everything they said exactly, because that will sound like parroting, which can become very irritating. We want to rephrase what they've said, using a few of their key words, and restate it in our own terms to make sure we understand the other person.

The third key is *reflective listening*. Reflective listening is reflecting back what the other person did *not* say—in other words, the emotions behind the words. You might say to somebody, "It seems like you're really frustrated." They may never have actually told you they were frustrated, but you recognize what they're feeling, and you can reflect it back to them. This will help them know that you really understand where they're coming from.

Now imagine for yourself how powerful it is if somebody else hears you, rephrases what you've said, and reflects back what you're feeling: when you know that other person hears and understands your thoughts. That is a huge step in openly communicating, discussing issues, and coming up with solutions.

You can combine the assertive skills by using "I" statements, asking the four questions, and employing your listening skills in order to move forward in almost any conflict.

Taming Toxic Types

Often in the corporate workplace, we come across many different personality types, a number of whom are very toxic. There's the angry bellower, the silent steamer, the drama queens, the great gossips, the lying deniers, and the crying culprits, and of course many more.

Let's go through each of these toxic types and understand where they're coming from so that we will have a chance to be able to move forward when we encounter them in conflict situations. Let's take our assertive communication skills and apply the "I" statements, the four questions, and active listening, rephrasing, and reflecting. Let's see how we can use these skills to deal with each of the different personality types.

> **Toxic Personality Types**
> - Angry bellower
> - Silent steamer
> - Drama queen
> - Great gossip
> - Lying denier
> - Crier

Say you happen to be dealing with an angry bellower, who gets angry and loud. Of course everybody can have a bad day, and an angry bellower might need an opportunity to blow off a little steam. It can be very effective if we simply give them an opportunity to do so. Give them an opportunity to vent. They'll be more likely to be ready to move on to a productive conversation.

When somebody is so angry that a productive conversation is impossible, we might be tempted to tell them to calm down. But to them, those are fighting words, meaning "escalate; get angrier."

So we go back to "I" statements and say, "I need thirty minutes." You may well be thinking, "*I* don't need thirty minutes; *they* do." We can't say that, but we can say, "I need thirty minutes." It's very important to give the bellower a specific amount of time; otherwise, they're going to feel that we're blowing them off and avoiding or ignoring the conflict. If we give them a specific time—about thirty to sixty minutes is usually appropriate—they will know you're ready to talk about it. By saying, "I need thirty minutes," you're not telling them to calm down; you're telling them, "I'm going to take care of something right now, and then we need to talk." This will set up a positive atmosphere for the conversation.

What do you do about the silent steamers? You know these people: they're upset and you know they're upset, but they say nothing. How do you handle somebody at work who stays silent and shuts down in a conflict situation?

In many cases, it is possible that the person who is silent really needs the time to think; they want to take a few minutes to process the issue. Give them that opportunity. Sometimes it's just a few minutes while they're sitting there; sometimes you need to reschedule your meeting.

The other possibility is that the person is going silent in order to avoid conflict. They don't say anything. They shut down, so they're out of it. They don't have to participate. But that doesn't mean the conflict goes away.

If you ask somebody what they think about a particular situation and they go quiet, you may become concerned that they're shutting down to avoid it. It may make sense to wait however long it takes: they may really need thirty or forty-five-minutes. The catch is that we don't usually have that much time. Most of us can't even sit quiet long enough for somebody to talk: we feel we have to fill the silence. If we do, chances are that we will let them off the hook by talking, for them. If necessary, have something at hand that you can work on and sit there, working on your task. If they get up to leave, thinking the conversation is over, you can say, "While I'm waiting for you, please sit back down. Whenever you're ready, we can talk about this." This gives them a clear message that going quiet and shutting down is not a way to get rid of this conflict: you really do need to have this conversation.

Sometimes we have a drama queen, someone who goes over the top in a conflict situation. How do you handle that? First, recognize that for them, drama is normal and natural. If we're uncomfortable with it, it's because it's not our way of dealing with conflict: it's just a difference in behavior styles. If we can say, "It's OK; that's how they think and function and process, and I can accept that," it goes a long way towards handling the drama appropriately.

With drama queens, you can say, "I'm the kind of person who really wants to do a quiet, focused conversation." Here you've gone back to assertive communication. You said, "I." You didn't tell them, "You don't need to be so dramatic. Hey, calm down." Instead of telling them what to do (or what they're doing), you're simply setting your own boundaries. You saying, "For me, this is how I can handle it. This is what I need to do."

At that point you and the drama queen could agree on a process. You can say, "OK, how do we make this work for both of us? We have different styles and different approaches. How can we have this conversation in a way that works for both you and me?" You'll probably find that because you cared enough to ask how to handle the process, they're going to be more willing to work with you on setting one that both of you can follow.

What about the great gossip? They just want to talk, and they're spreading those rivers of chatter that lead to conflict, and you're afraid of escalation. One way to handle this when a gossip comes in is to say, "Thank you for telling me that. Is there anything that you and I need to talk about specifically?

What is your recommendation?" You're letting them know that you don't just want to gossip. If you need to talk about a particular situation, that's OK. If it's not something that you need to have a conversation about because it involves somebody else, you're letting them know that you're not going to participate in their gossip.

What do you do about a lying denier? If somebody's denying, contradicting, trying to argue about something, what's behind that? They typically want to pull you into an argument. And if someone pulls you into an argument, guess what? Both of you lose. Don't let it happen.

There are three steps for dealing with somebody who is denying or contradicting. The first step goes back to rephrasing. If somebody is lying or denying, you can rephrase what they're telling you. You say, "If I understand you correctly, what you're saying is . . ." using a few of their keywords and putting the rest into your own words. When you've finished, you say, "Is that accurate?" They now have the opportunity to clarify something if you have misunderstood.

If this person is actually lying, one of two things could happen. They could say, "This person's really focusing on what I'm saying and repeating it back to me." They can choose to correct themselves right then and there.

With somebody who is lying on a consistent basis, you may want to follow up your verbal conversation with a written email describing what you understand about the situation. If somebody's lying, it puts them on notice that you are very aware of what they're telling you now so that if something comes up later, you can refer to your initial conversation. It's a process of turning that person from lying to thinking,

"Wait a minute. This is going to come back to me." They may start making choices to be honest and clear.

So you start with rephrasing. After you've rephrased what the other person said and given them the opportunity to correct any possible misunderstandings, you can say, "From my perspective, this is what I see; this is what I think; here's what's happening." Then you give them an option. You say, "Now would you like to handle it by doing A or B?"

If somebody wants to pull you into an argument involving denial or contradiction, handling it this way keeps you from being pulled into the argument. You are rephrasing what they say, acknowledging what they're telling you, giving your perspective, and putting options on the table. You're not going to argue; it doesn't matter who said it or who did it. You want to move forward without an argumentative process.

Another possibility is a conflict with somebody who cries. The crier takes the situation personally and emotionally. What can you do? In many cases, you can simply let them use a tissue and continue the conversation: it's OK to keep talking. If somebody's crying to the point where you can't keep talking, you probably need to reschedule. Make sure that you're giving them the privacy they may need and you are being respectful of what's going on for them. Again, you don't want to put the conversation off indefinitely, because if you do, you might seem to be blowing off the problem instead of dealing with it. Instead, you can say to them, "I need to go take care of something else. I'm going to come back in about fifteen minutes; we can talk then." By doing it this way, you're saying, "I'm going to give you privacy, and I'm going to respect what's happening. At the same time, we can still have a conversation." This lets them know that you're working with them and you will be able to talk about it.

Six Steps to Conflict Management

Let's look at conflict in general, then walk through a very powerful and effective six-step process for managing it.

Here's a statistic to consider. When people go to court, over 60 percent of the time they walk out of the door of the courtroom saying, "I don't care what the judge just said; I'm going to do it my way." Time and time again, people go back to court over the same issues because they want to do it their way.

By contrast, when people go through mediation or facilitation by walking through these six steps, better than 90 percent of the time they not only resolve the problem but follow through with the resolution. So consider your odds: do you want to fight about it and let somebody else make your decision, or do you want to work through the issue?

Let's now go through the six steps and understand how to become an effective mediator.

Six Steps to Conflict Management

1. Make sure everyone is heard.
2. List all the issues.
3. Find multiple solutions.
4. List action steps.
5. Make a written agreement.
6. Destroy all notes.

1. Make Sure Everyone Is Heard

Step number one to managing conflict is make sure to give everyone a chance to talk. Each person needs to know that they've been heard and been understood.

If you're involved in a conflict, should you talk first? As you may remember from assertive communication techniques, we always acknowledge the other person before giving our own thoughts. It's important to let the other person go first. You may say, "Well, wait a minute, I'm involved too; I want to go first sometimes." The bottom line is, it's going to take work to let the other person go first; that's their natural inclination as well. If you try to go first, chances are, they're not really going to hear you and you won't have the opportunity to look for win-win options. Always let them go first.

If you're acting as a mediator between two employees who are in conflict, who should go first? The key here is to let them decide. Ask them, "Who wants to go first?" If they can't decide, flip a coin or use some other neutral way of deciding.

When each person is talking, it's very important to use all the listening skills we've discussed: actively listen, make eye contact, and be aware of what your body language is saying. Rephrase what the other person is saying, using some of their keywords and putting the rest into your own words. Give them the opportunity to clarify anything that you might have misunderstood, and reflect their emotions back so they can see and understand where they're coming from.

2. List All the Issues

After each person has had a chance to talk, the second step of the process is making *one* list of all the issues and deciding on the discussion order. That word *one* is key. Here's why. Generally in a conflict situation, each person involved is thinking, talking, and arguing about different things. Often the parties don't even agree on what they're arguing about.

What do we need to do if we're divided? If we have two separate lists of concerns, we will often get confused, because we're still on separate pages.

The first step in bringing the parties together is to have the conversation and look at options. Making a single list sets everyone up for this process. Everybody should put all of their items of concern on that one, single list.

In terms of discussion order, sometimes you can say, "Let's talk about this first," and you can go through and pick through the rest. Sometimes this isn't possible, so you may need a neutral or random way of deciding about the order, like flipping coins. In any case, you need to decide which items you're going to talk about first.

3. Find Multiple Solutions

When you have had the conversation about the issues, conflict management requires that each person generate multiple solutions. Step number three is generating those multiple solutions. Let's look at why this is important.

If you're involved in a conflict, your first solution is almost certain to be what you want or need without taking into consideration what the other party wants or needs. If you just think of that one solution and stop there, you will dig your heels in, believing that this is the only solution possible. If you're required to come up with multiple solutions, you're going to realize, "Oh, there's more than one possibility."

It can be difficult to generate multiple solutions. Sometimes as mediator, you'll say, "OK, that's the first idea; that's one possibility. What would a different option be?" One of the parties might say, "I don't know." Then you can look at them and say, "OK, how do I go from there?" If they say, "I don't know," you would say, "If you *did* know, what would the possibilities be?" You're sending the message that it's important to have multiple solutions, so continue asking: "You heard me, right?"

Even if these individuals do not want to come up with multiple solutions, it is critical to have them. You might even ask, "If you asked another person—your best friend, the boss, whoever—what do you think they would say? What would they recommend?" Continue asking questions until you generate multiple solutions. Do this with every person involved.

4. List Action Steps

After you've developed multiple solutions, you need to sort out which solutions you will go with. In some cases, it's easy to decide, but in other cases, we're not sure. What can we do, then, to narrow down the solutions, eliminating the ones that we're not going to consider?

We can look at the possibility of combining solutions or taking part of one solution and part of another, and working through what those solutions really could be.

Once you know what solutions you're going to go with, step number four is to make a list of action steps and a timeline.

Here's an important point about action steps. If we say, "We need to communicate more," is that an action step? Not really, because a week from now, when we're back arguing, we don't know what this resolution meant. We don't know what it looks like, and we don't know how to make it happen.

Action steps must be specific, and they must be measurable. We've said, "We need to communicate more." OK, how do we make that happen? "We schedule meetings." OK, how frequent will the meetings be? "Every two weeks." OK, which day of the week? "Let's do Tuesdays." OK, what time? "We set meetings for every other Tuesday at 11 o'clock in the morning." Now we have a specific, measurable action step.

Action steps for solutions must also name the person or persons responsible for each step. If there's a time limit, note that as well: "Kathy's going to do X by Y time." We know exactly what this action looks like, and we can hold Kathy accountable to it as well.

5. Make a Written Agreement

Step number five in the conflict management process is to decide if a written agreement is appropriate. Once the parties involved in a conflict have done all the talking and worked out what they're doing and what the steps are, it's necessary to ask, "Do we need to have a written agreement for this? We're having the conversation. Have we handled it?"

This decision will be made by the people involved in the conflict. If they decide to have a written agreement, obviously it has to be written out. If they decide not to, that's their choice as well.

6. Destroy All Notes

Step number six is to destroy all notes. People are sometimes puzzled by this requirement. In conflict management, it's important that whatever you say in mediation is really going to stay there. You set it up right at the beginning. This is so important that not even a judge can subpoena a mediator. In certain court cases, attorneys or professional counselors have to give up privileged client information. You cannot bring a mediator in for this purpose. It's that important. Federal and state law both protect the mediation process so that everyone involved knows it is really confidential: there is no record-keeping.

Some may ask whether human resources must keep documents. In most cases, the mediator is obliged only to say that the meeting took place. That's it.

Destroying the notes tells the people involved that you really do care about the confidentiality and that it's OK to openly discuss what is going on.

Sample Cases

Let's look at some examples of applying the different skills we've been discussing to some conflicts.

The first one: Imagine being involved in a conflict personally. Have you ever had a situation where someone else who's not your boss or supervisor is telling you what and how to do something? This can be a complex situation. Let's see how we can apply the steps we've discussed.

If someone is telling you what to do and they're not your boss, you start with your assertive communication techniques. You're going to acknowledge what they're saying. You're going to let them know that they've been heard and ask to share your own perspective. You'll make sure to use "I" statements. You're not going to attack them, and you're not going to use the word *you*. You'll make sure all of your listening skills come into play.

Start with assertive communication techniques.

Say someone tells you, "You need to do that report." You're looking at them, thinking, "Wait a minute. You're not my supervisor. Who are you to tell me what to do?" but you're not going to say that. You're going to say, "If I'm understanding you correctly, you're telling me that I should be doing this report." Then you rephrase what they said. Then you're going to say, "Can I share my perspective on this? Because I know what my supervisor wants me to do, and that report is not on my agenda."

You don't tell them, "You're right, I'm wrong," or, "I'm right, you're wrong." You simply state the matter from your own perspective.

If the other person continues to say, "No, you need to get it done," you're going to say, "Let's talk about this. What do I need to know? What is the concern or issue from your perspective?"

You get out a paper and pen and write down a note. "OK, so you're concerned about this; you're worried about that. Tell me: what else?" Then you say, "OK, let me list my concerns as well," and you jot them down: "I'm concerned about making sure my boss is happy with what I'm doing and making sure that I complete the tasks that I've been assigned to." You list those issues.

Then you say, "OK, given these different concerns, which we both have, which one do you think makes sense for us to talk about first?" You can use your conflict management process informally and ask the other person, "OK, what do you think the possibilities are? That's one option. What other possibilities? What could be another? What do you think my boss would recommend? What do you think my boss would tell me?" You continue asking questions so that they give you multiple solutions, and do the same thing for yourself. You also have to make yourself look at different options and possibilities to make sure you're open to more than one solution.

After you've done that, if it's obvious which way to go, then you say, "OK, here are the action steps. How can I handle this?" Then you go into the four questions: "Where is it right now?" You've had that part of the conversation. "Where do we need to go? And how can this problem be prevented in the future?" "What actions do we need to take to get there?"

This person tends to come to you and tell you what to do. How can you prevent this from becoming a concern in the future? Guess what you're doing? You're empowering them to figure out how not to give you instructions if they're not your boss. So instead of you telling them, they reach that conclusion themselves.

To continue the process, do you need to have a written agreement? Yes or no? It depends. If it's the first time, chances are no. If you've had conversations multiple times, suggest, "Let's work something out. Let's write it down."

Then everyone tears up any notes they have made during the conversation. The only thing that's written down is the agreement you've developed. That's the conflict process.

Two Arguing Employees

Let's take a look at applying this process with two employees who are arguing. What do you do? How do you handle it? What steps will you take?

As the supervisor, you are going to act as a neutral mediator in this conflict. It's very important to stay completely neutral, because if you're not, you suddenly become part of the problem. If you're not neutral, it's not going to work.

How do you stay neutral? In mediation training, they teach what are called the "four nos."

- No opinion. Never give an opinion.
- No sides. Do not take sides.
- No advice. Do not give the parties advice on anything.
- No solutions, because if the mediator gives a solution, it doesn't come from the contending parties, and it won't work.

If you make sure to follow the four noes, you can stay neutral. Let's take a look at an example.

Two people that report to you are arguing over how to organize the workplace. Where are the files to be placed?

> **The Four Nos of Mediation**
> 1. No opinion
> 2. No sides
> 3. No advice
> 4. No solutions

Where is the computer to be set up? What about the desks, chairs, and other furniture?

You start out with step number one: everyone gets a chance to talk. You ask them, "Who would like to go first?" If you decide who goes first, that's taking sides. If they can't decide, simply flip a coin.

When the first person is talking, you are using all your listening skills: actively listening, rephrasing, reflecting back any emotions.

When you turn to the second person, it's their turn to talk. If you've ever been involved in a conflict, you'll know that the tendency now is to start arguing about anything and everything the first person said. That's not what you're looking for. At this time, you simply need to hear the second person's perspective: what they think and feel.

If you turn to them and say, "Don't worry about what the first person said," they're going to do the exact opposite and worry about what the first person said. You don't want that to happen. Instead you tell them what you *do* want. You turn to the second person and say, "Pretend I haven't heard anything up to this point, that I really don't know anything about this. In your own words, tell me what's happening."

That way you can truly focus on this person's words, again using all your listening skills: actively listening, rephrasing what they're saying, and reflecting back their emotions.

At this point, each person involved sees that they've been heard and understood, There's another benefit here as well. When the first person is talking, chances are, the second person doesn't want to hear it: they're not really focusing or listening. But when you rephrase and reflect back what one person is saying, the other person can hear you. They can now hear the person they're arguing with, because they hear it through you. Both of them are now more likely to start to understand what's going on. This is a big part of having them work out the conflict.

With step number two, you make a list of the issues. Say, "OK, you tell me what you think the concerns are." One person may say, "I want the file cabinet here." How do you list that as an issue or concern? If you write down, "Putting the file cabinet here," that's not really an issue: it's one person's solution. Instead, you write as the issue, "The location of the file cabinet." You're neutralizing the concern and opening the door to multiple solutions.

The other person might say, "I think the monitor should be located over there." You do the same thing: write down, "Location of monitor screen." This provides everyone with a list of issues that can be discussed without stating direct answers.

Let the two parties decide which issues they want to talk about and in which order. Sometimes they can't even agree about this. Sometimes they say, "We don't agree on the discussion. We'll flip a coin, and each person chooses the next topic." Give them that option, but let them choose.

Now you move to step three: generating multiple solutions. You might say, "OK, we're talking about the location of the file cabinet. What do you think the possibilities are?"

One employee says what they want. You ask for multiple solutions. After that person has given you multiple solutions, you need multiple solutions from the other. You say to that person, "Well, what do you think the possibilities are?"

"Well, I think it should be over there."

"What's another option?" you ask. Then, "What's another, and another, and another?" until you have multiple solutions from both individuals.

Now you say, "Of these multiple solutions, which one seems most likely?" They may agree right off the bat, or they may say, "She wants this one, but I want this one."

"OK, let's eliminate solutions that we're not going to consider." You then slowly go through the solutions in a process of elimination. If you don't get all the way down the list, you can say, "We're down to these two possibilities. Let's set this issue aside and come back to it. We can move on to another issue."

Sometimes the two employees will hit on a compromise: "OK. If I could put the monitor screen here, you could put the file cabinet there." You start combining solutions, tying issues together, and letting them have some give-and-take.

The other possibility is that you go through the issues and they generate solutions. Sometimes it becomes clear to both of them: "Hey, this is really a better answer. The office is going to work best if we tie all of these together."

Now you go to step number four: listing action steps. In this example, it's fairly simple: "OK. So, you're going to set this up; you're going to set that up." But if the solutions are a little more complex, you dig in with questions. "How do you make that happen?" Again, determine specific and measurable actions.

Next you come to written agreements. In this case, maybe the only thing you need for a written agreement is a checklist. What is getting moved where? Who's going to do it? You don't need to have a lot of detail on the whole conversation, just a simple checklist.

Sometimes the conflict is a little bit more involved; it's about personality differences. They say, "We want a written agreement," and you start getting into it: "Here's what we're going to need to accomplish," and you go into more detail based on the needs of the people involved.

The final step, of course, is to destroy any notes other than the written agreement checklist. This lets the parties know you really do respect them and their confidentiality.

Group Conflict

Now let's take a look at a group conflict situation. Let's imagine that you have a group of employees who are angry at management because there's going to be a new dress code. What do you do in a case like this?

If it's a large group, with fifteen or twenty people or more, it is very difficult for each person to talk. You want to let the employees know that each person's going to be heard and understood; you're just being realistic based on the number of people involved.

In a case like this, you can have them get into groups based on their opinions. Each group selects a spokesperson.

After the groups meet, the spokespersons talk: that's step one.

Step two is to make a list of issues. You have a flip chart on the wall, and you write out the different concerns. You ask the groups for solutions, and you do the brainstorming sessions. You start narrowing down the solutions. Then you'll list specific action items on a timeline.

You might say, "OK, we need a new dress code. What are the possibilities for it to look like? What are the possibilities for a timeline for implementing it?"

In a case like this, it is very important to involve management and have them participate in this conversation. They will need to be open to the process and to some give-and-take.

You want to work with the employees to decide if there needs to be a written agreement. In this case, there probably is, to be incorporated into the company's policies and procedures manual. You should help them organize a timeline for implementing the new dress code. Any other notes, personal and on the flip charts, will need to be destroyed.

So you need to walk through the same steps in each case, whether you're involved in personal conflict or whether you're acting as a neutral mediator for other people.

We have already emphasized the key part for making this process work: ensuring that every single person involved knows that they've been heard and understood. That's extremely important for each of us as human beings. The other central point is that the parties involved decide on the solution instead of having a decision handed down from above or outside. The participants are the ones who have to make an agreement happen.

> The key part for making mediation work: ensuring that every single person involved knows that they've been heard and understood.

What are the benefits of effectively managing conflict? We know that conflict doesn't go away. It just keeps coming back and, without resolution, will simply grow worse in the long run. Conflicts reduce productivity, waste time, and generate frustration and anger. Besides, when we effectively manage conflict, we're showing the employees that we really do care, we're going to listen, and we're going to make the process work out. We can achieve amazing results when we apply these six steps.

Summary

In this chapter, we started with understanding conflict. We moved to adjusting to personality and effective listening skills. We dealt with taming toxic types in the workplace. Finally, we went through the six steps for conflict management.

SIX

Great Grammar and Painless Proofreading

As you know, correct grammar and strong writing skills is essential in your role as a business professional. Simple mistakes can reflect poorly on you and your company. This chapter is intended to help you strengthen your writing and avoid future mistakes.

We'll look at five areas: grammar rules; misused and confused words and phrases; sentences; fluency, style, and voice; and proofreading.

> ### Five Grammar Issues
> 1. Rules of grammar
> 2. Misused and confused words and phrases
> 3. Sentences
> 4. Fluency, style, and voice
> 5. Proofreading

Common Mistakes

First, let's take a look at using active instead of passive verbs. Contrary to what some people believe, passive verbs are not necessarily incorrect: they are just not as powerful as active verbs. As the name implies, with a passive verb, the subject of the sentence is receiving the action, for example, "The boss was irritated by Bob." But that statement is stronger with an active verb: "Bob irritated the boss."

Another instance: "Ashley is tired from working long days." This passive sentence is wordier and less powerful than its active equivalent: "Long work days tire Ashley."

Finally, "Bill was fired by the CEO." The active version is, "The CEO fired Bill."

A more complex example: "For the project to conclude within the projected time, it is urged that all members of the team arrive promptly to each work session," versus:

"In order to complete the project on time, all members of the team should arrive promptly to each work session."

The second sentence, written in an active voice, is more direct and much more effective. Including extra words and phrases in your sentences often clouds the meaning and can even weaken the sentence.

Let's look at two examples and compare their effectiveness.

First: "In my opinion, the cost of the project could be cut by 25 percent if fewer people worked on it or we tightened the timeline and completed it a week earlier so we can move on to the next project."

Second: "We can cut the cost of the project by 25 percent by decreasing the number of team members and moving the deadline forward one week."

Again, the second sentence is stronger, because we have cut out unnecessary words and begun the sentence directly rather than starting with, "In my opinion." This phrase and others like it, such as "I think" and "I believe," only weaken sentences and the overall tone of the writing.

Next we can discuss parallel structure: giving equal weight and coverage to equal elements in sentences. Take this example: "My goals this year include getting a pay increase, to become assistant manager, and to go on vacation."

> Parallel structure is giving equal weight and coverage to equal elements in a sentence.

This sentence lacks parallel structure. Even though all three elements are goals, they're not presented in a grammatically equivalent fashion. The first goal is introduced with "getting"—the gerund form of the verb *get*—while the next two goals are introduced with the infinitive verb form: "to get."

Look at this revised version: "My goals this year include *getting* a pay increase, *becoming* assistant manager, and *going* on vacation." This sentence uses the gerund forms of the verbs *get, become,* and *go* to introduce each goal, keeping the grammatical parallel nice and even.

While parallel structure may not seem to be terribly important in business writing, it is an extremely effective way to ensure that your writing is noticed. Good parallelism adds structure, polish, and clarity. Let's look at another example of an incorrect parallel structure.

"The client demanded a five-star hotel to be driven by a chauffeur in a limousine and dinners at the most expensive restaurants in the area during his stay."

Is this parallel structure? No. Let's look at the correct parallel structure and note the simple way in which we can bring clarity to this sentence.

"The client demanded a five-star hotel, a chauffeured limousine, and expensive dinners during his stay." We have simply changed the parts of speech and taken out unnecessary words to make this sentence much clearer.

Let's move on to the third grammar mistake: misplaced modifiers. A modifier is a word or phrase that explains or describes something in a sentence. Misplacing it can change the intended meaning of the sentence. Take a look at this example: "Tom only works on Tuesdays." This sentence misplaces the modifier "only" in a way that changes the meaning, indicating that the only activity Tom does on Tuesdays is work. Logically that is not the case.

> Misplaced modifiers can change the intended meaning of the sentence.

Look at this revised version: "Tom works only on Tuesdays." This communicates the intended meaning, which is that Tuesday is the only day Tom comes to work. (Wouldn't we all like to have it as easy as Tom!)

In grammar mistake number four, we will look at the apostrophe. An apostrophe indicates either ownership or a contraction of two words. For example, "The bone that belongs to Rover is Rover's bone." If Rover is angry at the cat, we can form a contraction and say, "Rover's angry at the cat." The apostrophe does not indicate the plural form of a noun—a mistake that people often make: the plural of *cat* is *cats*, not *cat's* or *cats'*.

Grammar mistake number five is run-on sentences. Two complete sentences must be separated by official end punctuation, such as a period, a question mark, or an exclamation point. Sometimes two sentence elements can be separated by a colon, and often two sentences that are closely related can be separated by a semicolon. A comma used to connect two sentences without a conjunction is never correct and is termed a *comma splice*, as in the following sentence: "John went home, he was tired." You could separate those two sentence elements using a period, a colon, or a semicolon. If you have a series of complete sentences in a bigger sentence, you should probably rewrite it to avoid the sprawling sentence, which we will cover below.

Number six is a style that some people think indicates strong writing, but it doesn't: sentence sprawl. You might think of it as one big rambling sentence that seems never to end. Have you ever met someone who tends to ramble when they speak? Sometimes people write this way too. We're always waiting for a pause or an end so we can actually process the thought. Look at this example: "I think adjusting the schedule to accommodate the larger crowds this season due to warmer weather, will be better for a family fun day." Don't write this way. Keep sentences concise, particularly in business writing. You could write, much more concisely, "We should adjust the family fun day schedule this year to accommodate a larger crowd." If your audience asked you why, you could answer by mentioning the warmer weather. You want your sentences to be concise.

> You might think of sentence sprawl as one big rambling sentence that seems never to end.

Punctuation

Now let's move on to number seven: the misuse of the comma and other punctuation marks. Many people either overuse or underuse commas; we've already seen one example with the comma splice.

Let's keep in mind why we have the comma in the first place. The comma indicates syntax or the natural rhythm that words have on paper. But some people have no rhythm, and writing with pauses does not come naturally to them.

Let's take a look at some basic rules for commas.
1. A comma is used to set off an introductory prepositional phrase, as in, "With that in mind, we will proceed."

> **Basic Uses of Commas**
> 1. To set off an introductory prepositional phrase
> 2. At the end of a conditional clause
> 3. For parenthetical asides
> 4. To separate two independent clauses
> 5. Before the final item in a series
> 6. Before or after a participle introducing a dependent clause
> 7. After a date and a year
> 8. To set off the name of a state or country after a city
> 9. Between two consecutive modifiers
> 10. To set off phrases that explain a preceding word

2. A comma is used at the end of a conditional clause, as in, "When you are finished, we will go."
3. A comma can be used for a parenthetical aside. Commas go both before and after these remarks (although often it is better simply to use parentheses).
4. A comma is used to separate two independent clauses joined by what can be called the FANBOYS conjunctions: *for, and, nor, but, or, yet, so.* For example, "I am tired, and I am hungry."
5. A comma is used before the final item in a series, for example: "I like cats, dogs, and elephants."
6. A comma is used prior to, or after, a participle introducing a dependent clause. For example, "I began speaking, stating that John would be late." Or, "Using the com-

pany template, Margaret was able to type the spreadsheet easily."
7. Place commas after a date and a year: "We left May 14, 2013, and returned in July."
8. Use a comma to set off the name of a state or country after a city: Overland Park, Kansas.
9. Commas are used between two consecutive modifiers, such as, "The project will be very, very time-consuming."
10. Commas set off phrases that explain a preceding word: "She explains syntax, or word order, to the group."

Do not use a comma between the subject and its verb; between a verb and the object immediately following; between two parts of a compound subject, compound verb, or compound object connected by *and*, *or*, or *but*; or after a short prepositional phrase at the beginning of a sentence.

Semicolons are used instead of a conjunction when joining two complete thoughts to create a compound sentence, "Bring the report to the meeting; don't forget your tablet."

Semicolons also separate series of items with internal commas in order to clearly show the major separations between the items, as in this sentence: "She brought the report, which had been edited carefully; her tablet for the presentation; and the projector."

Colons are used primarily to divide major sentence elements, usually to call attention to whatever follows. They can formally introduce a list or an idea with expressions like, "the following," "as follows," "such as, or "these." The word following the colon is then capitalized when it is at the beginning of a complete sentence, but in lower case when it is not.

Business letters often use a colon after the salutation ("Dear Mr. Jones:") and after words like "subject" or "attention." Colons also are used to separate titles and subtitles; to indicate hours and minutes ("8:00 a.m."); with ratios; or to separate chapter and verse numbers in works such as the Bible ("Matthew 6:12").

Other punctuation marks, including quotation marks, dashes, parentheses, apostrophes, ellipsis points, and hyphens, are less problematic for most writers, but they can be misused. Check your reference guide for more information about punctuation.

As you can see, correct usage, punctuation, and spelling are vitally important to good writing. Always take the time to edit your work. Do not be afraid to ask questions or consult others about your writing. Not everyone is a skilled grammarian, so finding people who are well versed in editing skills could be your lifeline to better writing.

Pronouns and Antecedents

Let's move on to problem number eight: pronouns and antecedents. A pronoun, one of the eight parts of speech, is a word that replaces a noun in order to avoid repetition. The *antecedent* is the noun to which the pronoun refers. To avoid confusion, remember that the antecedent should come first in your writing. Keep the pronoun within the general proximity of the antecedent.

The antecedent should come before the pronoun.

Here are some examples of ambiguous pronouns: "Ben chased John through the park, and he broke his ankle." The pronoun fails to specify whose ankle was broken, Ben's or John's. You could correct it this way: "Ben broke his ankle as he chased John through the park."

Let's take a look at the next sentence. "When you see her, tell Ashley to be on time." Although this is a short sentence and it is easy to figure out that *her* refers to Ashley, you need to reverse that pronoun and antecedent. You could rewrite it this way: "When you see Ashley, tell her to be on time."

The final example here is confusing. "The second novel sold more than the first. Its ending left room for a sequel." What is the pronoun "its" referring to: the second or the first novel? A rewrite could sound like this. "The second novel's ending left room for a sequel, and it sold more than the first" or, "The second novel's ending left room for a sequel, which sold more than the first."

Problem number nine is subject and verb agreement. A verb must agree with the subject of the sentence in number, as in this easy example: "The ducks are in a row." Most of us realize this. It sounds incorrect to say, "The ducks is in a row," because that is using a singular verb with a plural subject.

Here are some trickier subject-verb agreement issues. Although we tend to give these words plural verbs conversationally, they are actually singular subjects and require a singular verb in writing: *each, each one, neither, either, everyone, everybody, anybody, anyone, nobody, somebody, someone,* and *no one.*

It is incorrect to say, "Everybody in the group agree." *Everybody* is a singular pronoun and should be paired with *agrees*, a singular verb. The same is true for the singular pronoun *neither*, as in this example: "Neither has reason to leave."

Grammar mistake number ten has to do with *me* and *I*, which are sometimes misused even by people with English degrees. Whenever you use *I*, it is the subject of the sentence: it is *doing* the verb. It *never* receives action from someone or something else. When you want to receive the action of a verb as a direct object, use the word *me*.

An example of *I* as the subject: "I proofread the document." An example of *me* as the direct object or the recipient of the action: "Judy fired me." But often when we have a compound direct object such as, "Judy fired Jim and me," people tend to think that they are grammatically correct when they say, "Judy fired Jim and I." If you get confused, take out that extra direct object, which will make it clear: "Judy fired I." That sounds silly, so that's a good test for correct use of *me* and *I*.

These are some of the most common grammar mistakes. This is not an exhaustive list, but you should notice and avoid these errors in your writing from now on.

Misused Words and Phrases

Malapropisms are words that sound similar to the intended word but mean something entirely different. While it's fun to laugh at these mistakes when they're made by characters in comedies, it is not fun to be laughed at for misuse of words or phrases.

> **Malapropisms are words that sound similar to the intended word but mean something entirely different.**

Let's take a look at eleven commonly misused words and phrases.

1. Should you use *fewer* or *less*? These two words mean essentially the same thing. You use the word *fewer* with things you can count: "I have fewer pens than Bill has." "My grandma has fewer teeth than I do." You use *less* with mass nouns or things you cannot count individually. For example, "Now that I have moved to the other side of the office, I experience less drama." "Since I took that organization class, I have less clutter on my desk."

2. Many people misuse the relative pronouns *which*, *that*, and *who*. The word *which* applies to things rather than people, as in this example: "The Jeep, which gets terrible gas mileage, is parked in the driveway." The Jeep is a material object, so it takes *which*. Here is an example of a usage to avoid: "Suzanne is the girl which keeps interrupting the teacher." It should be, "Suzanne is the girl *who* keeps interrupting the teacher."

The choice between *who* and *that* can be confusing, and the grammatical rules relating to it are complex, but here is the simplest practice for formal writing: *Who* is used for people; otherwise, use *that*: "Spike is the dog *that* bit me." The following example is best to avoid in formal writing: "Patrick hit the man *that* tripped him." You would rewrite this to say, "Patrick hit the man *who* tripped him."

On a more sophisticated level, the word *that* is used in a restrictive clause, while *which* is used in a nonrestrictive clause. An example of this is, "The client would like to discuss our newest line, *which* has the potential to increase sales." The second clause provides extra information: it doesn't identify which line the sentence is referring to and isn't essential to the first clause. You could change the sentence to, "The client would like to discuss the newest line," and leaving the entire clause out. Therefore, it is *nonrestrictive*.

However, in a sentence such as, "This camera is the only one *that* we sell," the clause "that we sell" is essential to the meaning of the sentence. If we took out that phrase, the sentence would not have the same meaning: "This camera is the only one." This clause is *restrictive*.

This practice even alters the rule given above, which stated that *that* is to be used for things and not for people. There are countless instances where *that* is used to refer to a person, as in an example from H.W. Fowler's classic *Modern English Usage*: "The Bishop of Salisbury is the third bishop *that* his family has given to the world." *Who* or *whom* would be completely inappropriate here.

Strictly speaking, *whom* is the objective case for *who*: the equivalent of *him* and *her*. It refers to a direct object, as in: "Yesterday, I saw John, *whom* Jim fired on Friday."

In common practice, *whom* is falling more and more into disuse, almost entirely in speech and increasingly in writing, so in most cases, it is not necessary to write *whom* even in cases where it is correct in the strict grammatical sense.

Some writers even say *whom* sounds affected and pedantic. Or you could recast the sentence above: "Yesterday, I saw John, *who* was fired by Jim on Friday."

3. *Lie* and *lay* tend to create confusion. The verb *lay* requires a direct object: something must receive the action. For example: "Lay that book on the table." The book receives the action. *Lie* does not have a direct object; it refers to an activity one does to oneself. For example, "Steve is going to *lie* down for a nap."

> The verb *lay* requires a direct object: something must receive the action. Lie does not have a direct object.

---

4. *Sit* and *set*. Dogs, cats, and people sit. For example, "My cat knows how to sit for treats." *Set* requires a direct object. Something is being placed somewhere. For example, "I set the cake on the counter."

5. Here's an often misused expression, which usually involves some attitude and emotion. Many people say, "I could care less" or, "I could care less what you think." If you think about it, this statement is literally saying that you *could* care less: I care some now and I am able to care less, so I do still have some feelings about this issue. The appropriate expression is; "I couldn't care less"; "I couldn't care less what you think." In other words, what you think doesn't matter to me.

6. *Nauseous* and *nauseated*. These two words do not mean the same thing. *Nauseous* refers to something that causes nausea. If you say, "I'm nauseous," you're technically saying, "I make someone feel like vomiting." Is this what you mean? If you mean that you feel like vomiting, the correct word is *nauseated*. You would say, "I am nauseated."

7. The extra S. These words do not have an S at the end: *toward, backward, upward,* and *anyway*.

8. *Versus* and *verses*. *Verses*, with an "es," is plural for the word *verse*, and is used in reference to lines of a poem or song. *Versus*, with "us," is a preposition meaning *against* or *in contrast to* and is used when talking about a conflict or a court case. It is sometimes abbreviated as *vs.* or *v.* (with a period).

9. This is an oldie, but these words are definitely still misused and confused far too often. *Accept*, with an A, means to *receive* something. For example, "I accept the position." It is a verb. *Except*, with an E, means to *exclude* something. It is a preposition. For example, "I like all dogs except pit bulls." A good way to remember this is that *except* and *exclude* both begin with an E.

10. This is another mistake that has been around for a long time but frequently continues to occur: *your* versus *you're*. *Your* indicates possession: something belongs to you. For example, "Your shoe is untied." *You're* is a contraction of *you* and *are*. For example, "You're the best mom in the world. An incorrect example is, "Your the best mom in the world."

11. *Irregardless* and *regardless*. While we sometimes like to believe that using longer words demonstrates intelligence, in this case it does not. The *ir-* in *irregardless* actually negates the word *regardless*, which already indicates lack of regard. *Irregardless* is never correct. Just say *regardless*: "Regardless of the weather, I am going hiking Thursday."

Sentence Fluency

You undoubtedly know what it means to be fluent in a language. It means you speak it smoothly with little effort. It sounds pretty, and it flows together.

Sentence fluency is the natural rhythm and flow of the words when a sentence is read aloud or read silently. A fluent writing style should sound and look effortless. The words of your writing should fit together well. Sentences should sound as if they are flowing together when read aloud. Sometimes you might need to rearrange words, choose different words with a better sound, or add or take away elements of the sentence. Just as you would take rough edges off a sculpture for aesthetic value, you need to do the same to your writing for the sake of fluency.

> A fluent writing style should sound and look effortless.

Strong sentence fluency includes variety in sentence patterns, the beginnings of sentences, and sentence length, as well as ease and natural feeling and flow when read aloud.

Let's take a look at some sentence patterns. We all use a variety of patterns when speaking; if you remember this, it should be easier to create sentences using a variety of patterns when writing.

The first and easiest sentence pattern is the plain old simple sentence. It consists of one independent clause. For example, "My grandma makes the best chicken soup."

If you want to mix it up a little bit, create a compound sentence with two or more independent clauses. Connect them with a comma and conjunction. For example, "I am hungry, so I am going to eat."

Step it up a little more with a complex sentence. This is an independent clause plus one or more dependent clauses. For example, "Even though I do not care for cats, my neighbor's cat is an exception because she acts like a dog." To feel like a pro, write some compound complex sentences, but not too many. You don't want to end up with sentence sprawl.

A compound complex sentence has two or more independent clauses plus one or more dependent clauses. For example, "Because I left work early without permission, the boss lectured me, but I was still paid for the entire day."

Did you know that most adults speak in compound complex sentences? Without overthinking it, try writing sentences down the way you would say them in a professional conversation, then go back and correct them for grammar.

If writing is a struggle for you, you may be a little intimidated by all the sentence pattern talk, but just ask yourself, "Can I carry on a conversation that flows?" If so, then you can write with fluency. Let's practice a bit.

> If you can carry on a conversation that flows, you can write with fluency.

Here's a boring, predictable, and elementary paragraph:

We already hired Joe Smith to build the supermarket. We are looking for someone better. We can pay Joe Smith 2 percent to release us from our agreement.

The sentence pattern is basically the same for all three sentences. Is anything technically wrong with them? No, but they're boring and basic. Take a minute and see if you can rework them into something more fluent. Here is one possibility:

Although we have already hired Joe Smith to build the supermarket, we have decided to expand our search for someone who better meets our needs. Mr. Smith has decided to release us from our current agreement for a 2 percent penalty.

Style and Voice

Maybe you want to be cool. You want people to think you dress well, have a hip hairstyle, and am with it. The bottom line is, you care what people think. You want them to find you unique. You may have a particular style, so someone may say to you, "Rose, that is something you would wear."

While many of us have a particular style of dress, decorating, and moving, not many of us think much about a unique writing style.

What does this mean? How can writing words on paper or typing them into a laptop have a style?

Style in writing simply refers to the word choice, sentence structure, and imagery a writer uses. Your style should be determined by your writing purpose. It will be different for writing historical fiction or poetry than it will be for business writing.

If you enjoy reading, you probably have a favorite author or two. Think of a novel that truly draws you in and engages you. Chances are, you can fluently hear the words and sentences in a natural cadence, which seems to flow as you read the story. You hear the voice in your head as you read. You do not have to work much to put the words and sentences together. Instead, you can focus on the content: the meaning of the words and the sentences.

Now think of a writer or a writing style that turns you off because of an awkward style, which does not flow. Some people dislike writing from before the twentieth century. The flowery, intentionally complex sentence structure that was in fashion then is a turnoff for many, who have to work too hard to hear it in their heads.

Keep in mind two writing styles—one you really like, and one that you find to be a turnoff—and copy the one you like. Is it OK to copy someone? Usually not, and often it's illegal, but it's all right in this context. Pick and choose some elements of your favorite author or writer and imitate and practice some of those elements in your own writing. Emulate the positive; identify what draws you into a writing style and incorporate some of it into your writing.

Copy a writing style that you particularly like.

Now think about the author or a style that you find to be a turnoff. Make a list of the elements that cause this writing to be uninteresting or awkward, and avoid using those elements in your own writing.

Take a couple of minutes to jot down your favorite writer. Write two specific elements you like about this writer's style. Then write down two specific elements or traits that you feel make writing bad or awkward. Hang on to your list, and remember these elements as you develop your own style.

Another important element of writing is *voice*. Voice is what sets you apart from other writers. It is your writing personality. Have you ever read a story or a novel that is written so that it seems you can hear the narrator speaking? One well-known example is the character Scout in Harper Lee's *To Kill a Mockingbird*. If you have both read the book and seen the film, you may find the narrator in the movie sounded almost exactly like the one you heard in your head while reading. This is due to the writing style of Harper Lee.

Your business writing voice will be more subdued than your regular voice. For business style and voice, you will need to determine your purpose. Is the communication external or internal? External communication will usually be more formal than internal. Usually the way you talk around close friends and family is far different from how you speak in a professional setting, and it is almost certainly different from how you write professionally. Be aware of the situation.

General guidelines for business writing include using shorter sentences, being direct, avoiding jargon and technical language, avoiding referring to yourself, writing from the company's point of view, and avoiding clichés and slang.

Vogue Expressions

Remember when you were a teenager? Depending on your age, you will recall the slang terms that made people seem cool (a slang term in itself) to others, ranging from "groovy" in the sixties to today's almost omnipresent "awesome." This is vogue language. Think of trendy, hip things you say because everyone else is saying them. Even if the words are different, they are basically the same as the teen slang from high school.

Here are some examples of vogue expressions that you should avoid:

- Don't even go there!
- Organic idea.
- At the end of the day.
- Throw him under the bus.
- On the same page.
- To the next level.
- Power through it.

- Touch base.
- Think outside the box.
- You do the math.
- Low-hanging fruit.
- Push the envelope.

Remember, it is easy to acquire a habit but difficult to get rid of it. Eliminate these words and phrases from your business vocabulary. You will come across as being more professional.

To sound professional, avoid vogue expressions.

Next, let's talk about empty and overused words. Empty words are devoid of meaning, and overused words are, as the name implies, words that you use too much. You have probably heard public speakers fill their speeches with vocalized pauses, such as *hmm*, *huh*, and *like* to fill space and serve no other purpose. Writers often do the same thing with empty and overused words. When you proofread, rethink these words, when you come across them. Think about whether or not they have purpose. Think about replacing them with something more specific. Here's a list of some common empty and overused words:
- Very
- A lot
- Generally

- Basically
- Specifically
- Currently

Think about how often you use these words in your writing and whether they are really necessary in every context.

Proofreading

These days, it seems we never have enough time in a day or a week for quality work, family time, and taking care of ourselves. We end up having to make choices about allotting time to various activities.

At the same time, no one likes to make mistakes. We know they are part of the learning process, and hopefully we do learn from them, but they seem to be a waste of time and a disappointment. Nevertheless, everyone makes mistakes, and catching our own mistakes is better than someone else catching them.

> Catching our own mistakes is better than someone else catching them.

The logical conclusion is that proofreading is not a waste of time. It will thus be helpful to plan time for proofreading and rewriting. Don't procrastinate. You do not want proofreading to be the step that you eliminate in a time crunch.

Here are some basic tips for better proofreading:
- Take a break between writing and proofreading.
- Proofread in blocks of time and in a quiet place.
- It can be extremely valuable to print a hard copy and use a pen when proofreading. It breaks routine and allows you to see the text in a different way.
- Read your text out loud and with expression. Nothing accentuates a mistake more than hearing it. Read slowly. Don't get in too much of a hurry to finish, or you will inevitably overlook errors. Does your writing sound correct when you read it out loud? If it does not, then check for correctness.
- Check for different kinds of mistakes separately.
- Be sure to check for spelling, overuse of words, sentence fragments, errors in agreement or word choice, or whatever mistakes you tend to make in your writing.
- Check for content and purpose, clarity, style, and parallel structure.
- Have someone else read your work and check for specific types of errors. Do you know that sentence fragments are a problem for you? Then have another person specifically check for sentence fragments.
- Use all your resources. If you are still not sure about correctness, look up the right answer. Use the Internet, using reputable websites, or consult a style book. Excellent writers use all available resources when editing and proofreading.

Summary

In this chapter, we've gone over some common grammar mistakes. We've learned several misused and confused words and phrases. We've discussed how to write fluently and incorporate unique style and voice to our writing. Finally, we've covered some tips for proofreading, so that your final copy is your perfect copy.

Hopefully, you've learned or been reminded of several ideas to make you a stronger business writer. At this point, you may want to make a list of the five most memorable ideas from this chapter and be sure to incorporate them into your writing.

SEVEN

Bad Email Habits

Email says a lot about you and your organization. In some cases, you may never meet someone face-to-face, relying exclusively on email and digital communications. Are you practicing appropriate email etiquette, or could your emails be hurting your reputation and your credibility? Mastering your email skills can go a long way toward forging the most professional image you can with potential clients, vendors, existing customers, and anyone else you communicate with.

In this chapter, we will address:
- The eight irrefutable truths of effective email
- Two surefire ways to ensure your emails are never read or taken seriously
- Planning emails
- Eleven documents and files that never belong in an office email
- How busy professionals really feel about jokes, quotes, and other e-clutter

- How to decide on the most effective format for your communication
- Cyberspace, confidentiality, and security
- What to keep, what to delete, and how to effectively file for future reference
- Eliminating excessive email in the office
- Easy email shortcuts that will save time and increase reader response

Eight Basic Truths

Let's review these eight truths of effective email communication.

1. Be sure your subject line is meaningful. Subject lines that do not clearly explain the purpose of the message can be confusing and might be taken for spam. In some cases, this could mean that your message will never even be seen.

2. Keep your message focused. Including many topics in one email or writing an unfocused, rambling message will cause your reader to lose interest or miss important information.

3. Limit each email to one or two topics.

4. Be sure to include all necessary attachments, but avoid attaching unneeded files. Numerous or large attachments can be difficult to sort through. They might keep your message from being delivered because it exceeds file limitations.

> ### Eight Tips for Effective Emails
> 1. Be sure your subject line is meaningful.
> 2. Keep your message focused.
> 3. Limit each email to one or two topics.
> 4. Include all necessary attachments, but avoid attaching unneeded files.
> 5. Use a professional tone.
> 6. Proofread all your emails.
> 7. Don't assume that any email is private.
> 8. Distinguish between formal and informal communication.

5. Use a professional tone, and avoid being too casual. Do not flame your recipients. (Flaming is the use of hostile language to anger or insult your reader.) Using a professional tone ensures that you are speaking respectfully, even if you disagree with someone. Show respect in all work-related communication.

6. Proofread all of your emails. It is essential to spell-check your writing, but it's not enough. Spell-check cannot catch misused words or words that are left out. You need to proofread to verify that your writing is error-free.

7. Don't assume that email is private. Any email can be forwarded, and all email is stored on a server somewhere for access later. Don't make statements in your email that you

are not comfortable sharing with coworkers, supervisors, or even strangers.

8. Distinguish between formal and informal communication. Informal communication should be severely limited in the workplace. It wastes time and diminishes productivity. Spending time on personal communication can also lead to disciplinary action. Keep your communication at work limited to business topics, and always show respect and restraint.

How to Guarantee That Your Email *Won't* Be Read

Your email recipients may ignore messages because they don't believe the content is important to them. They may believe the message is generic and sent to all employees, or maybe they just overlook it.

Two surefire ways to guarantee that your email is not read are (1) to leave the subject line blank and (2) to send an attachment with no explanation.

> Two ways to guarantee that your email is *not* read: (1) leave the subject line blank and (2) send an attachment with no explanation.

Emails with a blank subject line are often automatically sent to spam because the email application assumes they are unimportant or might even contain viruses.

The same holds true for attachments on a blank email with no explanation of the attachment's content. This is the primary way viruses are delivered, so most people delete messages like this without even reading them. Communicate clearly with your recipient so that he or she knows what you are sending from the outset.

Several types of files should almost never be sent as email attachments. Some of these might be self-explanatory, but others may need discussion in your office environment. To safeguard employee confidentiality, salary information, disciplinary documents, and phone transcripts should never be sent as email attachments. Additionally, jokes and personal files of any kind have no place in an office email. Tax information is especially important to keep private because it contains not only income information but personal information such as home addresses and Social Security numbers. Executable files such as Microsoft Office templates can be vehicles for Trojan horses and viruses. Finally, sexually suggestive or offensive images should never be sent as office email attachments.

Don't send unnecessary attachments or multiple attachments if fewer will do; only send what is needed. On the other hand, if an attachment is needed, make sure to include it. Don't make your readers email you for something that should be included in the email.

Planning Emails

In business, we send so many daily emails that we may forget how important this kind of communication can be. Business emails should be treated with the same gravity given to all written business communications. They need to be planned just as carefully as hard-copy memos, reports, and letters.

> Emails need to be planned just as carefully as hard-copy memos, reports, and letters.

When we take the time to plan out our emails, we can be more effective with our communication. We can avoid miscommunication and will usually get the response we need. Planning emails may take a little longer, but in the end, you'll find that you are able to get more done and will become more efficient with your communication.

Questions to ask yourself:
- Is email the best way to convey this message, or will it complicate the message?
- What is the main topic of my message?
- Who is my audience?
- Do I need a reply, and if so, when do I need it?
- Will I need documents, files, or reports from my recipient? If so, how long might it take them to gather these items?

By clarifying your objective in advance, you can make sure that your email accomplishes its purpose and your recipient clearly knows what you expect of him or her.

When *Not* to Send Email

Sending email has become so popular that we often do it without thinking, and this can lead to miscommunication, especially in business. Make sure an email is the appropriate form of communication. The first question to ask yourself is, should this communication be conveyed through email?

Consider this scenario: You have a conflict with a coworker. You decide you're going to email her to tell her exactly how you feel. You write a long message about the issues and how upset you are. You're rather harsh, but you feel you've been honest about your feelings. You proudly hit the *send* button in the heat of the moment. Feeling relieved, you are certain the situation will be resolved until you get the reply that is copied to your boss and several other supervisors. Your heart drops, and you are embarrassed as you explain to your boss what really happened.

Maybe an email is not the best way to discuss the conflict. In an email, your coworker can't hear your voice or see your facial expressions. Nor can she clarify her position or ask questions. In this example, a conversation by phone or face-to-face enables you both to reach an understanding without hurt feelings or further conflict.

Email might seem like the best option to handle an angry customer or coworker, because you can convey your message without interruption. Unfortunately, without vocal inflection or facial expression—and without allowing the recipient the opportunity to respond—your email could make a bad situation worse. In any emotional situation, it is far more effective to speak in person or over the phone: that way you can deliver the clearest message possible.

In fact, it's best to avoid sending emails when you're feeling any type of negative emotion like anger, irritation, or frustration. Emotionally charged emails almost always include words and phrases that will make you look unprofessional and irrational. Before you send an email about an emotional issue or situation, take time to put some mental distance between you and the message. Be sure to read the message again before sending it to ensure you have communicated in a very professional and objective manner.

> Avoid sending emails when you're feeling negative emotions.

Remember, all emails can be forwarded. So before sending an angry email, ask yourself if you want your email to be viewed by everybody, including your supervisor and other executives. If you feel you must write down your feelings, write the email and delete it without sending it. This will allow you to relieve the emotional pressure without making a bad situation worse.

Here are some other times when email should not be used: when you're sending a heartfelt thanks or an apology. Again, because email is only words without the tone, often even the sincerest email will be mildly received. Sincerity is the key in both of these situations. An email just doesn't convey the depth of emotion we need to effectively communicate these messages. If you want to sincerely thank someone, say it in person, write a note, send a small gift, or stand up at the meeting and say something nice about that person. If you need to apologize, do that in person as well.

Also avoid email when the subject is complicated. If it seems too complicated to write in an email, then email is probably not the best communication channel. Emails are not meant to be intense or intricate; talking is a better option.

Avoid email when you want to keep something confidential. What seems like a private conversation can become a public mess with the click—maybe accidental, maybe purposeful—of the *forward* button. Furthermore, email lasts forever; your status with the recipient of that email might not. So be careful.

Avoid emails with inappropriate content. The joke may seem funny to you, but one poor choice could cost you your job; it might also cost your employer a lawsuit. Almost 10 percent of employers have fired an employee for a non-work-related email. By one estimate, businesses lose over $650 billion every year due to unnecessary emails. So learning when and when not to send an email could not only make you more efficient but could also save your company significant money.

Any email—including those within your company, to a vendor, to a customer or to any business relation—can easily be forwarded. Moreover, it's never really confidential or private. Even if you are only using your company email, the company information technology (IT) department can track your emails. Company emails should never be used to discuss personal projects or private social plans. We've all seen the news coverage of public figures who inappropriately used business email to communicate private matters. This is a very dangerous position to put yourself in.

Keep in mind that in many areas of government, emails are considered public record. If an email is made or received in connection with the transaction of any public business, it is public record, regardless of whether it was created or stored in a private or a public system.

Whenever you send an email, you should assume that it is not private and may be seen by people other than the intended recipient. Carefully consider whether you really want your message to be available in writing for everyone to see.

Email is not appropriate for every communication. Knowing when to use email and when to choose another channel will help you avoid this bad habit.

What Do You Want to Accomplish?

The second step is to decide what you want to accomplish with your email. It's important to consider what you want the recipient to do with the message that you send. There are three specific purposes that an email can serve.

1. **To deliver information.** This email doesn't require response; it provides quick, simple, written documentation that you have conveyed the information.

2. **To request information.** When you're requesting information, it's best to be specific. Asking someone, "Do you have

the info I need?" is very vague and often leads to miscommunication. It's better to ask specifically what you want, such as, "Can you send me the sales report for June?"

3. To invite or request attendance. Email has become the preferred method of inviting people to meetings and events. When you're using email for this purpose, it's important to include the necessary information, like the date, time, location, and what invitees are expected to bring or provide at the meeting.

Three Purposes for an Email
1. To deliver information
2. To request information
3. To invite or request attendance

When you are sending your email for any of these three purposes, remember that email communication may not be instantaneous. The email could be delayed, the recipient could be unavailable, or the requested information may need to be assembled. If your request is extremely time-sensitive, you're probably better off using a more immediate form of communication. Always remember to build in waiting time when you're communicating by email.

That brings us to the next bad habit: using email for high-priority communication. Urgent matters are best addressed by in-person meetings or phone calls.

> Urgent matters are best addressed by in-person meetings or phone calls.

Who Needs to Receive the Email?

Step three of the planning checklist is deciding who needs to receive the email. Sharing information with all stakeholders is essential, but not everyone needs to receive every message. Excessive and irrelevant email can clutter an inbox and make it more difficult to notice important information.

Think carefully about who needs to receive the email. If it has possible future ramifications and your supervisor needs to be alerted, definitely include them. But is it really necessary to copy them on every email?

Decide if your email needs to go to one person, more than one person, or a distribution list. If it does need to go to a distribution list, ensure that everyone is on the list and everyone on the list really needs the communication. Avoid the bad habit of sending emails to everyone regardless of whether it's relevant to them.

Do You Need a Reply?

Step four on the planning checklist is to determine if and when a reply is needed. It is frustrating to send an email requesting information or documents and not get a timely response. This often occurs when we do not set clear deadlines. We may send a message asking, "Can you prepare the June sales report?" when we really want to say, "Please provide me with the June sales report by 5:00 p.m. Wednesday." The more specific you are in your request, the more likely you are to get an appropriate and timely reply.

The Subject Line

The subject line is one of the most important elements of an email. The subject line tells the recipient the topic of the email, and often how important it is. It's a bit like a headline in the newspaper. If the headline doesn't grab your attention, you're not likely to read the article.

Most business professionals receive many emails every day. If they took the time to read each one, they wouldn't have time for their actual work. Over 90 percent of people don't read all of their emails. They skim, categorize, and delete those that they deem not critical.

Because we rely on the subject line to help us pinpoint the important messages, subject lines are a must. They make the reader curious to learn more and tell them what to expect, yielding a higher open rate and a higher response rate. They allow your message to reach your recipient without automatically being routed to spam, and they greatly increase the chance that your message will be opened and read. They help people prioritize, organize, and sort their email.

For these reasons, you need to always include a clear and relevant subject line. It should be concise, specific, and understandable. For example, writing "Issues" might signify importance, but it's vague. Writing "Computer server issues" will give your recipient more information and also allow for better organization.

There are three reasons for taking time to craft a meaningful subject line: (1) It's easier for the recipient. They know what to expect. (2) Subject lines allow for tracking of the entire conversation even if it spans several days or weeks. (3) A clear, concise subject line will make it easier to search for specific emails later.

Here are some tips for creating an effective subject line:

1. Give the essence of the message. The first place to communicate the message is here. The clearer your subject line, the more likely your message will be opened, read, and answered.
2. Limit your subject line to fifty characters or less, and use the first four words for the most important information. Since most email programs limit the part of the subject line you initially see to fifty characters or less, information after that point may never be seen.
3. Skip unnecessary words. Boil your message down to the essence of what you're saying. Instead of "Following up on the meeting from Wednesday," it's better to write, "Follow-up, Wednesday meeting." Wordy subject lines make it more difficult to analyze the email's topic and importance. Keep the subject line specific and relevant.
4. Similarly, don't input the entire body of the message in the subject line, as in: "Joe, let's talk about lunch. How's Italian? Meet you at our place at 12. Bob." Not only is that wordy, but it makes it difficult to easily categorize that email.

5. Be precise. It's better to write, "The sales report due Friday" than, "The deadline approaching."
6. If you are requesting action, help your recipient by including this in the subject line. For example: "Meeting Friday; RSVP by Wednesday."
7. As already mentioned, a blank subject line almost guarantees that an email will be deleted without being read, even if it makes it to the inbox without being sent to spam.

The Effective Subject Line

In order to craft an effective subject line, follow these steps: Help your reader prioritize email by including a call to action in the subject. If the readers are required to respond or act, include, "Action required." If the email is only informational, it could be helpful to state that the message is "for your information" (FYI). If the action required is time-sensitive, assist your reader by including the deadline and the subject.

If you write regular emails about a similar subject to the same regular contacts, use a consistent format in your subject line. For example, "Weekly sales update, August 15, 2015." This makes for more predictable communication and allows the recipient to organize messages more easily.

Avoid improper capitalization. It's important to grab the reader's attention, but using all caps in any part of an email is equivalent to shouting. Conversely, using all lowercase letters suggests mumbling. The subject line of an email is still formal business and should receive proper spelling and punctuation.

A great tool to help organize emails is to use a status category. For example, Microsoft Outlook allows email to be categorized as "high priority," "normal," "low-priority," "personal," "private," or "confidential." These quick labels give the reader more information on the subject line. Avoid the overuse of "high priority" and "urgent" tags on emails. When all messages are tagged as "important" or "urgent," the reader starts to ignore them, and you become like the little boy who cried wolf: before long, no one pays attention anymore. Only mark emails with these tags if they really are urgent, important, or high-priority.

Two more bad habits to avoid in the subject line are being too vague and too general. If the subject line is very generic, like "Meeting," the reader will have difficulty prioritizing and categorizing the message. It also costs the recipient more time when trying to locate that communication later. Be specific, such as, "Friday, July 15 meeting."

Avoid being too casual in your communication. Be professional in your writing, especially on the subject line. "Hi there!" "Hi!" or "Hey!" could easily be routed to spam or ignored.

If you are sending an email to someone you have never met or you're writing an email for marketing, you need to work carefully to create interest. Good email subject lines can increase marketing results and open the door to new opportunities. For Warren Alderman of the GoDaddy domain register company, his carefully crafted subject line, "How I know you," drew him to the attention of the company founder. As a result, he landed the interview, was hired, and eventually became the CEO.

The more creative your subject line is, the more likely it is that your email will be opened. Here are a few tips for writing subject lines that create interest and curiosity.

1. Avoid sounding like spam. Anything that looks like spam will be routed to the spam folder and never seen.
2. Use the name of a referring person to facilitate an introduction, as in, "Referred by Jim Smith." This is very easy to do if you're on LinkedIn: just see who the recipient is connected to that you also know. Make sure you ask permission to use the referrer's name.
3. Use numbers, especially in lists. Lists are popular because they provide information quickly and concisely. Busy professionals like this. A good example is, "Five reasons you need to meet me."
4. Use more verbs and fewer adjectives. Instead of being too descriptive, the subject line should tell your readers what action to take. For instance, "Change the world in two minutes or less." This states the purpose without giving too much away.

Tips for Writing Subject Lines

1. Avoid sounding like spam.
2. Use the name of a referring person to facilitate an introduction.
3. Use numbers, especially in lists.
4. Use more verbs and fewer adjectives.

The subject line needs to grab attention while still stating the main message of the email. Taking time to craft an effective subject line can be the single greatest factor influencing whether your email is read or deleted.

The Body of the Message

The body of your email contains your main message. Make sure this message is clearly delivered and understood. The first key to a good email body is to ensure that your communication is professional and businesslike. Here is a checklist for an effective message body.

1. Be professional. Email is formal communication, so be sure to communicate professionally. Use an objective, neutral voice and standard business language. Construct a message with the same formality and care that you would use for a business letter.
2. Include a call to action so that the reader knows what you want. Place the call to action early in the message, and include deadlines. You will probably get a quicker response if you put the call to action on a separate line by itself, which allows the reader to quickly find what they need to do and respond.
3. Limit each email to one or two related topics. Including too many topics in one email is confusing and lessens the chance that each topic will be thoroughly read and understood. Following the thread of the email and tracking responses are much easier when topics are limited to one or two related items. If you have multiple topics to address, sending multiple emails will increase the chance that all messages are read.

> **Tips for Writing an Effective Message**
> 1. Be professional.
> 2. Include a call to action.
> 3. Limit each email to one or two related topics.
> 4. Format your email for easy reading.
> 5. Limit attachments to those that are needed.
> 6. Avoid being too casual.
> 7. Spell out what you're saying.
> 8. Proofread and spell-check your emails before you send them.
> 9. If the message is informational only and no action is needed, be sure to state this.

4. Format your email for easy reading. Use bullets and paragraph breaks, and make sure your message is not overly lengthy. Include context and responses so the reader doesn't have to guess at the topic.

5. Limit your attachments to those that are needed. Too many attachments can increase the size of your message and may make the email too big to send.

6. Avoid being too casual by using overly familiar salutations such as, "Hey there," or making jokes. Jokes can backfire. They could accidentally offend your reader. Being boring or serious may not fit your image of yourself, but being offensive can get you fired.

7. Spell out what you're saying. Using abbreviations or emoticons can be confusing and distracting to your reader.

8. Proofread and spell-check your emails before you send them. Even if your software checks for spelling and grammar automatically, take an extra minute or two and review the message: spelling and grammar check cannot correct missing words or the wrong word. If the message is important enough to write, it is important enough to proofread. The proofreading process should include checking for proper capitalization, proper punctuation. Using all caps or all lower case is not appropriate and can send the wrong message. If you're writing your message from a mobile device, this step can take a little extra time, but clarity and professionalism should not be sacrificed for convenience.
9. If the message is informational only and no action is needed, be sure to state this. If you need action in response to the email, be sure to state that as well.

Proper Formatting

Use proper formatting for your message. This will make it easier to understand and quicker to read. Here are some formatting tips to increase the clarity of your communication.

1. Limit the length of the body of your message to six lines or three short paragraphs. Breaking up the message into small paragraphs makes it easier for the recipient to digest. Writing one long paragraph with no breaks is a common formatting mistake. This makes it very difficult for the reader to clearly understand the message. An action request can easily be missed.

2. Use an extra line space between paragraphs. The extra white space makes the message much easier to comprehend.
3. Use bullets to delineate separate items, such as items that you are requesting. Bulleted lists are easier to read than dense paragraphs.
4. Try to limit the message to one screen. This is especially vital for reading a message on a mobile device such as a smartphone or tablet.
5. Failing to include context in an email response can cause your email to be misunderstood. For example, your supervisor asks, "Are you going to the meeting on Friday?" and your response is, "Yes." The recipient, who gets many emails a day, may not know what question you're responding to, especially if you have not included the thread in the message. It's better to respond with, "I will attend the meeting on Friday. Thank you." This may take longer to write, but it will save time in the long run by avoiding confusion.
6. Consider that not everyone has the same sense of humor or the same political or religious outlook. Busy professionals want to address their daily tasks without unnecessary distractions. It's best to avoid sending or forwarding any jokes or cartoons.
7. As mentioned before, too many attachments are confusing. They can make a message so big that it's undeliverable. You can also place information on a server and send a link. This will reduce the chance that the email will be rejected by the server. Before sending your message,

double-check that you have included all needed attachments.
8. Before hitting the *send* button, check the spelling, grammar, and punctuation to ensure that your email is well written and understandable. Also check for tone. Read your email out loud. If you're concerned that the tone could be misinterpreted, have someone else read it. This is critical if the email is of a sensitive nature.
9. Finally, fill in the TO, CC, and BCC lines. We'll discuss these next.

TO, CC, and BCC Lines

When your email will be read—if it's read at all—can depend greatly on the sender. If an email is from your supervisor or someone you know, you're more likely to read it and respond quickly. One way to become more effective when you're sending your email is to look at the TO and FROM checklist.

First, fill in the TO line last. This recommendation might seem odd, because we naturally start at the top of the email. We fill in the TO line, the CC (the copy line), and the BCC (the blind copy line). Then we fill in the subject and start typing the message.

But filling the TO line last will keep you from inadvertently sending the message before you're finished, because it cannot be sent without a recipient in the TO line. Complete the TO, CC, and BCC lines only after you have completed your message and proofed it.

> Filling the TO line last will keep you from inadvertently sending the message before you're finished.

Below the TO section is the CC, or the carbon copy function. Make sure your CC list includes *only* those who need the information. Research suggests that over 40 percent of staff time is wasted on reading internal emails such as CCs. Another report, by the cloud-based email management company Mimecast, says that 61 percent of emails received at professional email accounts are nonessential. That's over half of the emails we receive. You can help improve office productivity by reducing unnecessary CC messages.

Another type of CC to consider carefully is the CC to the supervisor. Some people think that when they send a request for information, sending a copy to that person's supervisor will motivate the person to respond quickly. But this doesn't necessarily ensure a prompt response, and it even could cause resentment. By copying the supervisor, you're basically asking for assistance in getting the information, and the supervisor may not welcome this responsibility. Moreover, the recipient may take offense. Only copy the supervisor if you really do need their assistance or if the supervisor needs the information.

It's a good idea to CC your supervisor only the information that you know needs a response. If they need to know about something else, send a separate email rather than including them on the CC. Make an agreement with your supervisor on how to use email effectively.

Be especially careful and considerate with sensitive or confidential information, unless a supervisor needs to know for human resource purposes. Maintain your recipient's trust by keeping private information private.

The difference between a CC, the carbon copy, and a BCC, the blind carbon copy, is that CC line can be seen by all recipients while the BCC line is invisible. The BCC line allows you to send email to multiple people without their knowing who else is getting the email. It is good to use the BCC when sending an email to numerous people who don't necessarily know each other. If, say, you volunteer for a nonprofit organization and send emails to hundreds of people, make sure that all email addresses are on the BCC line, because you don't want everyone in the group to see all addresses. That's an appropriate use for the BCC line.

> **Use the BCC when sending an email to numerous people who don't necessarily know each other.**

However, consider your decision carefully before using the BCC line on an email sent to an individual at work. Because the BCC function can be seen as secretive, it can also be seen as manipulative.

REPLY ALL should be used when you're confident that all recipients on the email will be interested in the content of your response, or they need to be aware of what your reply contains. Unless your message is truly meant for everyone, limit your reply to the sender only. Reply to the sender only if you are asking for more detail on the message, responding with your individual action items, or sending a negative or sensitive response. If your message addresses performance or HR issues, consider discussing that matter in person instead of sending the email.

Conversely, if there's a group conversation going on via email—say a communication that's going on in your team—make sure to use the REPLY ALL function. Maybe it's an email that's sent amongst your team. Just clicking REPLY in this instance could create a bottleneck, forcing the recipient to forward your email to everyone, or it can cause people to ask why you haven't responded.

If you find yourself caught in an email conversation loop where both participants continue to be confused, make an effort to talk to that person instead. While email is a powerful communication tool, it can be imprecise and sometimes inefficient. Like many things, email can a blessing and a curse.

If you're forwarding the link to an article, always provide a summary. It's a bad habit to paste a link in an email that says, "Read this" or says nothing at all. Let your recipient know what you are sending, and provide information on the content.

Finally, let's discuss email signatures. A signature line is recommended, but it should be concise. It should contain only necessary contact information: your name, your company name, your position, your phone, and your email address. Don't include personal information, and don't include quotes unless there's a compelling reason. Remember that business communication should be objective, concise, and efficient. This rule also applies to your signature line.

Managing Your Inbox

If you don't have a specific system for managing emails, you could spend more than half your day sorting them. Many workers spend an average of three hours per day on this task. That's about 40 percent of your work spent just on email.

You can be more efficient and productive if you establish some simple strategies for managing your inbox. The first step is to establish a regular time to read and respond to emails rather than responding to each email as soon as it arrives. Depending on the nature of your business, decide on how often you need to check emails. For many, checking email two to three times a day is enough. A good schedule to adopt is checking email in the morning, right after lunch, and right before the end of the day. Clearly, in some roles you will have to check email on a more regular or frequent basis, especially if your business uses email as the main communication tool. As with all of these strategies, use your judgment and experience to determine what is most effective and efficient for you.

> Decide how often you need to check emails.

Another good strategy is to automatically file emails in customized subfolders by adding filter rules that match certain criteria, such as sender address or subject content. You can sort email into different folders and automatically archive messages. You can also reject emails containing viruses. You can block unwanted senders and sort or reject unsolicited junk mail.

If you're going to be out of the office for an extended length of time, set up your automatic reply so that others know you are away. It's frustrating to request information within a specific time frame and not receive it. Using the out of office alert will let your associates know how long you'll be out and whom to contact if they need immediate assistance.

One common habit that reduces efficiency is using notifications to alert you every time a message arrives. These alerts can be distracting and can draw your attention away from the task at hand. Set up a schedule for checking messages, and turn off the notifications.

Another bad habit is checking emails as soon as they arrive. By instantly answering all emails, you may set up unrealistic expectations about your ability to respond. On the other hand, be sure to respond in a timely manner. Checking email three times a day and responding to all communication within twenty-four hours will generally allow you to manage your time efficiently while still being responsive to everyone. If an email requires research or additional time before a response can be sent, email your sender with that status update.

Finally, using your inbox to store all messages can create the equivalent of an electronic junk drawer. Having hundreds or even thousands of emails in your inbox will make it increasingly difficult to find and respond to messages that you want. Learn to use rules that logically sort your communication.

The ultimate way to reduce inbox clutter is to have a system that enables you to quickly sort and organize your emails. One great way to organize email is to employ the 4R system to determine the most effective way to file emails.

The Four R System
1. Refer
2. Recycle
3. Respond
4. Record

The first R stands for *refer*. If the email is requesting information that you cannot provide, then refer the email to another person. Do this first to allow the new recipient time to respond in a timely manner.

The second R stands for *recycle*. If the communication is junk mail, a chain letter, or some unbelievable offer, send it to the recycle bin without even opening it. Never open attachments from someone you don't know unless you are confident the source is safe.

The third R is *respond*. If you have the knowledge and time to respond to an email immediately upon reading it, do so. Clear it from your task list, then file the message appropriately and enjoy that small feeling of accomplishment.

The fourth R is *record*. Is the message something that you need to save, file, or refer to in the future? If so, put it in the appropriate folder. Sometimes you want to leave a message in your inbox as an immediate reminder that action is necessary. Most email programs have a flag option that will highlight the message as a reminder.

Using a folder structure for filing email will make it easier to sort your messages. Folder structure makes it easier to search for past emails. Instead of scouring your entire email system, you can simply search in one particular folder.

If you don't currently have a filing system or you're unsure of how to create one, use broad categories related to the type of response needed. Examples would be action items, waiting, reference, and archives. This type of folder system can also create an informal to-do list for the day. If these categories sound too simplistic for your needs, you can set up a much more detailed system. For instance, you could create a folder for every project that you're working on or create a folder for each of your clients or sales reps.

The Out of Control Inbox

If your inbox is out of control, it can feel overwhelming to start sorting it out. Some email inboxes contain over 10,000 emails. That has to be stressful.

Here are some suggestions. Start by creating an old email folder. Move everything in your inbox to this folder. You're not deleting anything. You're just moving things to subfolders in order to start with a clean inbox.

To deal with a cluttered inbox, create a file for old mail and put everything from your inbox into it.

Next, sort the emails by date, and move messages still requiring action back into your inbox. Third, decide how you will handle emails from today forward. Create a sorting strategy and begin using it. Don't be concerned with the messages in the old emails folder. You can always search it for emails that you might need.

Most of us feel overwhelmed by email at times. Although it is a great communication tool, you'll need careful management to prevent waste and inefficiency. By managing your email instead of letting it manage you, you can increase your effectiveness and significantly boost your productivity.

Summary

This chapter discussed subjects including the eight irrefutable truths of effective email; ways of ensuring that emails will be read; writing the subject line and the body of the message; correct use of CC and BCC; avoiding inclusion of offensive content. We also covered confidentiality and security; effectively filing for future reference; and easy email shortcuts that will save time and increase recipient response.

EIGHT

Business Writing and Editing

In this chapter, we'll discuss writing for business and the workplace and how you can improve your writing skills.

Good writing is good business. In the workplace, communication is crucial for the business and its employees to be successful. Writing can make or break a reputation. You've undoubtedly seen signs, billboards, or even business documents that have not paid careful attention to spelling or grammar. Maybe you laughed a little or rolled your eyes, but those mistakes negatively impact the public's perception of that organization. Something as small as a misplaced apostrophe or a misspelled word can reflect poorly on the writer and the company. This is why good writing and good editing are important for you and your employer's reputation.

> Something as small as a misplaced apostrophe or a misspelled word can reflect poorly on the writer and the company.

To begin with, regardless of the type of writing, always use a considerate tone. Put yourself in the recipient's shoes. If you were to receive a correspondence that was rude, curt, or without careful consideration for you as the reader, would you continue to want to do business with that person or company? Think of the last time you dealt with the employee of a store or restaurant. Even if your order was wrong or the employee couldn't find what you were looking for, your frustration was probably diminished if they were helpful, courteous, and considerate.

In writing, this sort of consideration is shown in using expressions like *thank you* and *please*. Being considerate is one more way to make your business look good.

In this chapter, we will begin with understanding your purpose and your audience for your business communication, followed by organization of ideas and effective sentences. Next we will look at editing, spelling, usage, and punctuation. Finally, we will review tips on professional presentation and publication.

Formal and Informal Writing

A good writer always knows and writes for his or her audience. Understanding the audience's biases and backgrounds is crucial for choosing the correct words, phrases, and tone. Since there are various types of business writing, it is important to tailor your writing not only to the audience but to the purpose of the writing. For example, if you know your supervisor does not have time to read lengthy reports or emails, you want to adjust your writing out of consideration for their time. You might provide shorter documents with bulleted points rather than multiparagraph essay-style reports. Likewise, if you were to write a research paper on infant sleep patterns for your company and a very detailed report with statistical data is required, you would want your writing to be as specific and thorough as possible.

We can break workplace writing into two categories: formal and informal. Formal writing includes proposals, business letters, case analyses, reports, and business plans. Informal writings, which we will cover first, include emails, memos, meeting minutes, and even instant messaging. In your career, you will have to write both formally and informally, so we will study both.

Informal writing should be brief and concise. When we receive minutes from a meeting or an office memo, we want the main ideas only. Writing that is too content-heavy is often disregarded. Consider the last time you got an email from a colleague that had many paragraphs and little white space. Did you read the entire email thoroughly, or did you skim it to look for the important points and file it away for later?

Informal writing should be brief and concise.

When writing sentences, make them short, declarative sentences. There is no need for complex or compound sentences in most business writing, especially the less formal version. A sentence that reads, "The new policy will alter some benefits" is much more effective than, "The new policy with its far-reaching effects will alter some benefits, but you should not notice them immediately."

Use plain, specific English. There is no need to write the word *utilize* when you can write the word *use*. Use direct statements that get to the point. White space is important in informal business writing—sometimes almost as important as the writing itself. You want the recipient to find the information quickly and easily. Using bulleted points, short sentences, or even key words and phrases is much more effective than a large number of long paragraphs. We rarely have the time for this kind of writing while at work, and we must read it on our own time, or it gets lost in the to-do pile. Get to the point quickly and simply by providing the necessary details without too many words. Shorter paragraphs with white space between them do not overwhelm the space: we are able to see key words and phrases more easily and note their importance by their location within the document.

Outlining the information can help your colleagues or clients find the main points quickly. Most types of word processing software include options for outlining or bulleting information, enabling the writer to easily create memos and outlines using templates and formatting tools.

When writing memos, make them able to be read quickly and efficiently. Use only one main idea per paragraph. Avoid complex phrasing. Elegant writing is not necessary in workplace writing. Avoid jargon when writing to larger audiences outside the office. In memos, this sort of word choice is pretentious and unnecessary.

Make your primary point first.

Finally, make your primary point first. Fill in next with necessary detail, but do not spend time leading up to your idea for the sake of enticing your reader. No one has time for that in the workplace.

Emails and Instant Messaging

Let's look at some other types of informal writing: emails and instant messages. With today's portable, pocket-size technology, many of us work around the clock these days. We receive and send emails and text messages at work and at home, in the evenings and on weekends. In order for our messages to be taken seriously and read as they were intended, it is important to pay attention to word choice and tone.

We went into detail about emails in chapter 7, but some additional points may be useful. The workplace is not the right place for joking or suggestive comments. Many companies offer workshops and seminars on appropriate workplace behavior, but in texts, instant messages, and emails, it is often easy to forget to use a professional tone.

Keep your messages on topic. Using sarcasm, suggestive words, and innuendo is not appropriate, even when the coworker is a friend. Remember the golden rule of messaging: nothing in in-house email is ever completely erased.

You may use company jargon and technical terminology, but always use the clearest possible language. Organize your emails into levels by using headings and subheadings to steer your reader, and use bullets or daggers to show levels of depth or importance. Writing in all caps, as we've noted, is the written version of shouting and should only be used for extreme emphasis. Use other formats, like italics and boldface, to catch the eye of the reader. Avoid emoticons in workplace writing. Even a little smiley face can be seen as unprofessional. Additionally, avoid exclamation points. While you may be excited about a staff meeting, curb your enthusiasm when writing a reminder email.

> Writing in all caps is the written version of shouting.

Finally, some experts in business writing recommend limiting your emails to five or fewer sentences. While this may be a challenge, it can also be quite beneficial when trying to grab and hold the reader's attention long enough to get your point across.

Instant messaging has quickly become one of the best forms of communication in the workplace. The benefits include instant feedback or answers to problems and questions, as well as increased productivity, because a coworker does not have to pick up the phone or walk down the hall to speak to you. However, it is important to remember some tips so your message doesn't get you into hot water.

First, be respectful of your colleagues' time and availability. Do not carry on lengthy conversations via instant messages when you should be working. This wastes not only your time but that of your colleague and company. If your respondent doesn't respond immediately to an instant message, they are probably busy at the moment or away from the computer. Do not allow your frustration to cause you to forget to be considerate.

Likewise, respond in a timely manner when someone sends you a message. If you are going to be away from your desk or computer for a moment during an instant messaging session, let the other party know or simply type "BRB" for "Be right back," and let your respondent know when you've returned.

In instant messaging, just as in all other forms of informal writing, use appropriate and respectful language. The company's instant message service is not your personal account. What you write should be courteous, respectful, clean, and workplace-appropriate. This is not the vehicle for spreading office gossip or dirty jokes. Be sensitive to others. Just as in an email, sarcasm and attempts at humor are not always taken the way they were intended. It is difficult to detect tone in an instant message, so these attempts should be kept for your personal time and accounts.

Finally, know when *not* to send an instant message. Do not use it (or email) if you need to speak to someone about a sensitive issue. Pick up the phone, or, if possible, speak to the person face-to-face. Instant messaging is great for informal instant feedback, but not for delicate issues that require a personal conversation.

Formal Writing

Formal writing includes business reports, analysis, plans, and proposals. In all formal writing, be thorough and exact. Like with informal writing, it pays to get to the point quickly, but in formal writing, main ideas must be supported. For example, a proposal must include all requisite parts: the objective, rationale, project description, benefits, and cost analysis. In order to reach your target audience and provide enough information to get your proposal approved, you must be thorough. Too often, proposals are rejected or postponed for lack of sufficient information. Nevertheless, concise statements are still warranted in this type of writing and are appreciated by the reader.

Your formal writing must also answer the reader's biases and needs. A thorough report would be specifically written to answer the audience's potential questions. For many employers or clients, cost is the number one issue. Provide a specific cost analysis using exact numbers, down to the penny if possible. Your description and rationale should be specific too.

> Formal writing must answer the reader's biases and needs.

Business Letters

Business letters are formal documents and can be used to apply for jobs (cover letters) or deliver information. Always tailor your business letters to provide the main idea in a concise manner. It is possible that the reader may only skim your letter for key information. Get to the point quickly and organize the letter so the reader can find the information they are looking for efficiently. Do not hesitate to use industry-specific language in order to demonstrate expertise, but take care not to be confusing.

Some templates for business letters can be found in office software, but it is always best to design your letter to fit the purpose and the reader. Business letters should be constructed in the standard format, which includes the date, addresses, salutation, body, and closing. The date belongs at the top of the page. The return address is followed by the recipient's address, also called the *inside address*. Skip a line between each address.

Next comes the salutation. Skip an extra line after the inside address. It is customary to use "Dear" when the recipient's name is known and "To whom it may concern" when the name is unclear, or you may use the title of the recipient if it is going to a specific department.

Next is the body of the letter. Double spacing is unnecessary here. Nor do you indent the first word of each paragraph, as you would in other multiparagraph writing. But insert a line space after each paragraph.

Following the body is the complimentary close. Keep it friendly but professional by using "sincerely" or "with regards" as your closing statement. Leave a space for your signature if it will be printed and signed, and then your printed name and title. You may want to include your company name if the letter is not written on the company letterhead. If there is an attached document, be sure you type "enclosure" or "enc." at the end of your letter a couple spaces below your printed name and title.

Understanding your audience and the purpose for writing are the most important aspects of business writing. They will help you determine what should be written, and how, before you ever begin. Remember, be concise, use clear, direct, and specific language, and always be considerate.

> Be concise, use clear, direct, and specific language, and always be considerate.

Organization

Picture the structure of a building. What is its most important part? The foundation. Without the proper foundation, the building will fall down. Similarly, writing starts with a solid foundation. A sturdy frame will hold everything else together. Designing the right structure will make your document professional and credible.

Consequently, you must first identify the main idea, which is the foundation. The main idea may be in the title or heading of the document, or it could be found in the subject line of an email. Always identify the subject or main idea clearly. To use a previous example, a report on the sleep patterns of infants might be titled, "The Sleep Patterns of Infants: Birth through Twelve Months."

The subject line is the source of a common mistake in workplace emails. Instead of "FYI" or "Thought you might be interested in this," the subject line should contain the main topic. "Cost analysis for property acquisition" says much more than "The report you asked for." Use specific key terms in subject lines and as headings and titles.

Next, support the main idea effectively. If you must include data in your report, organize it in a logical way. Thoughtful organization of supporting ideas makes the document easier to read and understand. The report on infant sleep patterns might be organized by specific months to show the progressive changes, or by specific sleep behaviors and their corresponding ages.

For a report analysis or other types of longer writing, organize ideas into paragraphs that follow a logical pattern. Group your subtopics and support these with evidence, examples, and explanation. Begin with a topic sentence, followed by a subject and wrapped up by a concluding sentence or statement. Effective sentences emphasize ideas in a logical and complete way. Like paragraphs, sentences carry a main idea and a complete thought.

Sentence Structure

The following tips will help you organize and write effective sentences. First, put an important idea at the beginning or ending of a sentence. For example, "The overall cost of the project will include local and state licensing fees." The subject is the overall cost. Putting the main idea at the beginning of the sentence will immediately draw the reader's attention to it.

> Putting the main idea at the beginning of the sentence will immediately draw the reader's attention to it.

Second, arrange items in order of increasing or decreasing importance. An example of this type of sentence could be: "The project's costs will include local and state licensing fees, materials, and labor." Since labor is typically the most expensive cost in any project, followed by materials and then fees, this sentence's ideas are arranged by increasing importance.

The sentence could be rearranged to read: "The project's costs will include labor, materials, and licensing fees." This loses none of the impact but simply changes the sentence arrangement from increasing to decreasing importance.

Another tip to increase the effectiveness of your sentences is to repeat key words and phrases. In marketing and advertising, this is a well-known and widely used practice to capture the audience's attention. Think about how many times a business's name or product is used in a radio or television ad. Repeating key words, especially the name of a business or product, means that the reader or audience is more likely to remember it.

Lastly, set off ideas with punctuation. Dashes, colons, and commas are effective in breaking up the sentence and emphasizing ideas. For example, "The project's cost with labor, materials, and fees included is within the projected budget—and below our competitors' estimate."

Another way to write concisely is to limit prepositions. Instead of writing, "The team came up with a new idea," write, "The team generated a new idea." Or instead of, "We will figure out the costs," use the word *determine*: "We will determine the costs." Likewise, avoid overused prepositions that tend to cloud the meaning or make the sentence too wordy. Instead of writing, "The meeting on June 1 to discuss the budget," you could write, "The June 1 budget meeting." Using fewer words makes an impact.

Effective writing is varied in structure. We often overlook this strategy. Consider the following two sentences, and decide which sentence is more effective.

First: "The cost will include labor, materials, and licensing fees. The cost is 10 percent lower than our competitor's estimate. The cost, as you can see, is well within the requested budget."

Note that "the cost" is repeated three times at the beginning of each sentence. Let's look at a more varied sentence:

"Lower than our competitor's estimate by 10 percent, the cost of the project includes labor, materials, and licensing fees. As shown, it is also well within the requested budget."

Again, the second group of sentences, which uses fewer words and is varied in its beginning, is much more effective.

Editing for Sentence Problems

One of the most important steps in the writing process is editing and revising. It isn't enough to type out a quick email or document to share with your colleagues. Just because you've corrected all the spelling mistakes with the help of a spell checker does not mean your document is ready for publication. The first step in editing is to revise the big ideas. Check your organization and make sure your ideas make sense in their current state.

> One of the most important steps in the writing process is editing and revising.

Once you have the major components of your document revised, it is time to begin looking at more specific details. Start with sentence construction. The following tips will help you check and edit common sentence problems.

It may seem elementary to look for sentence fragments, but today's abbreviated modes of communication, like texting and instant messaging, make it easy to overlook such mistakes. We often speak in fragments as well, so naturally we tend to overlook them. A sentence fragment attempts to convey an idea but falls short, because it is missing one element of the sentence such as the subject, verb, or the complete thought.

These two sentences are fragments: "Because the cost was too high. Sharing the workload between two teams."

Let's correct them: "Because the cost was too high, we went with another vendor. We will be sharing the workload between the two teams."

This second version completes the thought with the help of a subject and a verb. Now it is complete in structure and form.

Like fragments, run-on sentences often plague our writing without our notice. Consider this sentence: "The team leader finished her report early before she left for the meeting but since she still had four additional memos to complete she returned to her office and worked until midnight."

This sentence says a great deal without punctuation or breaks in thought. Let's look at one way to correct it: "The team leader finished her report before the meeting. Considering that she still had four memos to complete, she returned to her office after the meeting and worked until midnight."

Notice that we have broken this sentence up into two. We have also added a comma between the two clauses in the second sentence. Today's average sentence contains approximately sixteen to eighteen words. Going above twenty may create problems in comprehension. Take careful notice of your sentences to be sure they are clear and concise.

Another common sentence problem has to do with modifiers—the words and phrases used to describe a noun or a pronoun. A dangling modifier creates confusion, because it does not specifically refer to the noun or pronoun being described. The result can be confusing, as in the following sentences.

"Walking through the office, the computer was turned on." Here it sounds as if the computer was walking through the office, and the sentence sounds silly.

Another instance: "Checking the payment stubs, several errors were spotted." In this sentence, we don't know who spotted the errors or checked the payment stubs, so this sentence is confusing.

Here are the corrected sentences.

"Walking through the office, Mary stopped to turn on the computer."

"Checking the payment stubs, the clerk spotted several errors."

Both sentences are much clearer now, because they have clearly identified the subject.

Like the dangling modifier, a misplaced modifier can make a sentence confusing, because the modifier is not located near the noun or pronoun it is describing. For example, "She was employed for two years while going to school as a salesperson." Was she employed for two years while she was going to school, or was she going to school to be a salesperson? Let's move that phrase closer to the pronoun to clear up this confusion: "While going to school, she was employed as a salesperson for two years," or, 'She was employed as a salesperson for two years while going to school." Both versions are much clearer.

Fixing modifier problems is usually as simple as changing the word order of the sentence. Such minor edits can substantially improve the writing.

A similar issue is dangling prepositions. We commonly dangle our prepositions when we speak, but in writing it is considered informal slang and far too casual to write a sentence ending in a preposition. For example, in a conversation, you might ask, "Who should I give this report to?" But in writing, the correct phrasing is, "To whom should I give this report?" As previously noted, *whom*—the objective case of *who*—has increasingly come to sound stiff and pedantic, and many writers are avoiding it altogether. If you don't want to come off sounding like a stuffy English teacher, you could ask, "Who should receive this report?"

When we write, we too often use the reflexive compounds of *self* incorrectly as a subject. However, a reflexive pronoun cannot serve as the subject of the sentence or even the object. It must refer back to another pronoun that has already been used in the sentence.

Let's look at an incorrect usage of the reflexive pronoun: "John and myself will attend." It should be written as, "John and I will attend."

The sentence, "Send a copy to Mary and myself," is also incorrectly stated, and should be corrected by changing *myself* to *me*, as in, "Send a copy to Mary and me."

For pairing ideas, use *either, or* or *neither, nor*. Make sure you use each pair correctly. For example, "They asked him if he wanted either the day off or extra pay. He wanted neither the day off nor extra pay."

As you edit for better and more accurate sentence structure, remember that sentences are part of a paragraph, and correct paragraphs contain the following components: a topic sentence, naming the main idea being discussed; support materials such as facts, details, specific examples, evidence and opinions that support the main idea; and a summary sentence that concludes or finishes the main idea. You can remember this by recalling a simple formula; *preview, state, review*. Preview the main idea, state the support for it, and review the main idea once more.

Editing your paragraphs and sentences for clarity and correct structure may not seem like an enjoyable way to spend

> **A Formula for Paragraphs**
> 1. Preview the main idea.
> 2. State the support for it.
> 3. Review the main idea once more.

your time, but the effects of writing clear, well-written sentences could mean a sale, a pat on the back, or a promotion. Little nuances in sentence construction and flow can make all the difference in your writing.

Editing for Spelling and Usage

Next we will discuss editing for some of the most common errors in spelling and usage. These issues are often regarded as nitpicky, but their misuse can be detrimental to your writing and your career. Good writing goes beyond good ideas. Clarity of expression and thorough editing are essential. Spelling and grammar errors denote a lack of care. Editing for these problems is always time well spent.

In the first place, please go back and review the sections relating to spelling, punctuation, and grammar.

It is a good idea to have a list of commonly misspelled words handy. Many educated adults misspell the word *definite*. Similarly, *college* sometimes becomes *collage*, and *a part* becomes *apart* far too often.

Keeping a dictionary and thesaurus handy is always helpful. Dictionaries often give more than one correct spelling for a word, but the first one listed is the preferred one, if you are unsure.

Learn specific spelling rules. This might mean finding and using a grammar book or reference guide like those used in college composition classes.

When you have finished drafting a document, print out a hard copy and read it. Then read it again, this time backwards. This will prevent you from skimming it too quickly as you proofread.

Usage issues are so commonplace they often get their own section in a grammar reference guide. Expressing yourself effectively and clearly depends upon the words you choose and how they are used.

Here are some other problematic words in English (there are many more). Again, it would be a good idea to have a grammar reference guide and a dictionary at your desk for professional quality writing.

There are four meanings to the similar sounding words *affect* and *effect*, which causes much confusion in writing.

Affect (as verb). The verb, spelled with an A, means *to influence* and is the most common use of this word, as used in a sentence such as, "The new payroll policy will *affect* employee salaries in a positive way." Here *affect* means to influence salaries.

Affect (as noun). The same spelling of *affect* as a noun means *feeling* or *emotion*. This is comparatively rare, but it is used often enough to cause confusion in spelling and usage. For example: "Elizabeth showed little *affect* during the exercise." In speech, *affect* as a noun is accented on the first syllable—*af*fect—whereas as a verb, it is pronounced with the accent on the second: af*fect*.

Effect (as verb). The spelling of the word with an E, as in *effect*, dictates the meaning as well. As a verb, *effect* means *bring about* or *cause*, whereas, as we have seen, *affect* means *to influence* or *implement*. Note these two sentences:

"The new health insurance will *effect* changes in the benefit expenses of some employees."

"The new health insurance will *affect* the benefit expenses of some staff members."

Effect (as noun). *Effect* as a noun—its most common usage—means *result* or *outcome*, as in, "What *effect* will the delay have on the project's completion?

Notice these subtle yet important variations in a set of words that are spelled and pronounced similarly.

End punctuation marks—periods, question marks, and exclamation marks (which we know to use sparingly)—are not usually an issue in most writing. However, commas, colons, and semicolons tend to cause problems for most people who do not write professionally. Therefore, we must make a conscious effort to learn the rules of punctuation and use them correctly. We noted some basic points in chapter 6, but we can go into more detail here.

Periods are used for ending a complete sentence that is a statement or after an indirect question, as in "Mr. Flynn asked where the cost analysis was." Periods are also used in some abbreviations. If you are using an abbreviation with a period at the end of a sentence, do not add another period. For example, "It was my first business trip out of the U.S." Despite the abbreviation, there's just one period at the end of the sentence. Not all abbreviations contain periods, so it's best to consult a dictionary if you are not sure.

Professional Presentation

For a document to be ready for publication or presentation, it must be *proofread, polished,* and *professional*: the three Ps of writing. Let's look at these three in greater detail.

> **The Three Ps of Writing**
> 1. Proofread
> 2. Polished
> 3. Professional

As we have seen, checking for spelling, usage, and punctuation is key to effective finished products. Often we spend so much time drafting a document that we do not give ourselves enough time to proofread effectively.

A good general rule: spend as much time proofreading and revising a document as drafting it. It's almost always needed. Allow others to read your writing before publication or presentation. We often miss our own errors because we know what we mean to say, and that is usually what we see on the paper or screen. As stated before, print out the document so you can read it offscreen. You can catch many errors this way too. Read it slowly, and read it forward and backward.

Read the document aloud. Does it sound good? Are there missing pauses where the comma should go? Is there a missing period or a sentence fragment? You can catch several errors simply by reading out loud to ourselves or an audience.

A good presentation or document will be a polished one. Once the errors are corrected, make your document stand out. Unless it is in a form used by the company with very strict formatting rules, give the document a little style. Make presentations stand out through the use of larger fonts for important ideas or headers. For important words and phrases, use boldface, capitalization, and italics. Cartoonish clip art is not appropriate for any work document, nor are emoticons, as mentioned previously. However, the use of color to delineate columns in a spreadsheet, the use of boldface type to convey important terms or statistics, and the use of larger, more prominent font size for headings can be effective when polishing your documents.

Be extremely attentive to the final appearance of the document, which will influence the reader. Document presentation will determine the reader's opinion of the writer's professionalism.

> The final appearance of the document will influence the reader.

How the information is arranged on the paper is important as well. As discussed previously, white space in a memo or email is beneficial for drawing the reader's attention to the writing's main ideas. Likewise, whatever the writing, effectively arranging the words, paragraphs, tables, graphs, and charts on the page gives the reader a better focus. Keep your margin standard. Do not decrease the margin size to fit everything on one page. Filling up white space with words can cause the reader to lose focus and your writing to look sloppy. Use double spacing whenever possible, except on letters. A little extra white space on the page allows the reader to track the words and sentences more easily.

Although the use of italics, boldface, and even capitalization is effective in highlighting specific words and phrases, do not make the mistake of using nonstandard fonts for the overall document. Choose a standard font such as Times New Roman, Calibri, Cambria, Arial, or Century for your professional writing. Script fonts or casual fonts like Comic Sans are not professional and should not be used in workplace writing. Keep your font size standard: eleven or twelve points. Anything smaller makes the document more difficult to read, and anything bigger is unnecessary.

Professional presentation folders or covers can show your readers the care and consideration you have put into your writing. Sold at any office supply store, presentation covers help keep the pages of your document clean, crisp, and organized. These are typically used for multipage documents or reports. Make sure the covers are free of cutesy elements such as flowers or ornate designs. Keep them simple, neat, and clear of extraneous detail. If you are including graphs, tables, or charts in a presentation, use color and professional-style graphics. Make those graphics large enough so the information is easily identified and used.

Finally, if making multiple copies of the document for presentation, make sure everything in the document is standardized, from the organization of the pages to the direction and placement of the staples. This will enhance the professional appearance of your writing.

Presentation is almost as important as the document's contents, but it does not take the place of the writing itself. Always make sure the content of your document is solid, well written, and edited carefully before considering it for presentation or publication.

> Presentation is almost as important as the document's contents, but it does not take the place of the writing itself.

Summary

Writing is not easy. Published writers often shake their heads at their own published work and think they could have done better. Consequently, it is a skill at which one must work hard in order to see improvement.

While workplace writing is different from novels or journalistic writing, many of the same skills apply. In this chapter, we went through the essentials of business writing. Beginning with audience, tone, and ideas, we moved toward organization of paragraphs and sentences; then we went on to details such as spelling, usage, and punctuation. The ultimate objective is to create a polished professional document.

CONCLUSION

Practically everyone has to work with other people. And working with other people means communicating with them. Much unhappiness and many mistakes in the workplace arise out of poor communication. As a result, no matter what your job may be, you can greatly improve your work—and your life—by mastering basic communication skills.

This book has introduced you to the most important aspects of effective communication. If you master the material here, you will go far toward promoting your own success—and eliminating a great deal of personal dissatisfaction.

As we've seen, communication takes a number of forms:

Verbal communication has to do with actually talking with others. Your word choice, even in the simplest conversations, will have a great deal to do with your impact on other people. We've observed, for example, that saying "you" in certain contexts—"You made a mistake"—can in itself come across as an attack. We've also seen that the SEER method—whereby you start with a *summary* of your point, *expand* upon why you think the way you do, give an *example* to back up your argument, and *restate* your point—can do a great deal to persuade both coworkers and people in your personal life.

Word choice is important, but it's not the only factor in verbal communication. You also have to take into account paraverbal communication, such as your tone of voice or even the words you choose to accent in a spoken sentence, which can completely alter the power of your message.

Then there's body language—another major part of communication that goes far beyond the words you use. Do you have a diffident, weak body posture, or do you convey confidence and assertiveness? These details will carry great weight in the results of your communication.

Much of interpersonal communication—even the most ostensibly businesslike—relies on emotional impact. We've seen that the key point for dealing with emotions when interacting with others in every context is being able to manage your own emotions.

Since you won't and can't manage your emotions simply by repressing them, you have to find another approach. One of the most important facts that we've explored is that *emotion follows thought*: the easiest and most effective way to deal with your emotions is to change the thoughts that produce them. We've gone through a number of techniques for mastering this process.

Another major theme of this book is that communication doesn't move in one direction only: it's at least as important to truly grasp what the other person is saying and feeling.

As a result, we've paid a great deal of attention to *effective listening*: trying to grasp clearly and accurately what someone else is saying without silently trying to prepare a reply or a refutation. We've gone through a number of tips and techniques for being a more effective listener. We've also discovered that effective listening is one—but only one—central factor in conflict management and resolution.

The second major aspect of communication is through the written word. Mastery of writing may well be the single most important skill that will advance your success and reputation. As with verbal communication, the basic goal is to convey an impression of competence and professionalism. Correct grammar and spelling (although often dismissed these days as mere pedantry) are absolutely vital to how you and your company are perceived.

Over the past few decades, email has become by far the most popular means of communication in the workplace. We've seen that it's just as important to master the right tone in email as it is in conversations. You need to convey professionalism and courtesy in every message you write. You also owe it to the recipient (and yourself) to make your email as clear and comprehensible as possible, preferably in a space of two or three paragraphs per email. Every detail of email communication will influence whether your recipient even reads it. We've seen the importance of a clear and concise subject line and of carefully targeting recipients so that everyone who needs to read your message does so—and that it does not go to people who are not involved.

Finally, we've discussed the importance of emotional intelligence (aka EQ). It is your ability to recognize and manage your own emotions, recognize and respond to the emotions of others, build effective social relationships, and ultimately support your success at both work and home.

One key factor in developing emotional intelligence is awareness. It's wise to pay constant attention to the impression that you're conveying in every detail—including your attire and workplace decor—instead of assuming that people will just have to take you as you are. Emotional intelligence also involves sensitivity to the messages that others are conveying and responding to them courteously and effectively.

We've all heard the Golden Rule. The great playwright George Bernard Shaw suggests an emendation: "Do not do unto others as you would they should do unto you. Their tastes may not be the same."

Being aware—not only of yourself but of others—may be the single most important part of true communication. Courtesy—trying to respond to others as they would like to be treated—is the second.

If you master these simple principles, you will go far in mastering communication and advancing in whatever milieu you choose.

www.ingramcontent.com/pod-product-compliance
Lightning Source LLC
Chambersburg PA
CBHW072152070526
44585CB00015B/1113